To Darell.
Phil 1:6
Blessings!.
Dr. Rawson "Buff" Carlin

GREATER THAN A HIGHER POWER

Addiction Recovery Yesterday, Today, and Forever

by

Dr. Rawson "Buff" Carlin

GREATER THAN A HIGHER POWER

Addiction Recovery Yesterday, Today, and Forever

Dr. Rawson "Buff" Carlin

First Printing: December 2020

50% of all profit from the book will be donated to non-profits ministries such as Teen Challenge and missions.

ecarecounseling.com or greaterthanahigherpower.com

Dr. Carlin is available to speak at your church, school, civic group, or conference event. Call (704) 883-6599 for booking information.

Foreword by Rev Don Wilkerson

This is an important and hopeful book to contribute on how to find freedom from addiction. Dr. Carlin has both the experience of living in addiction and finding the Highest power in Jesus Christ to permanently overcome his personal enslavement to drugs and go on to receive treatment training. He is well qualified to share how others can also find what he found in The Higher Power. This book contains a major message on addiction recovery and the reader will find the investment of the time reading it worthwhile——and possibly life challenging. In addition, this is an in-depth look at addiction from many treatment modalities. It is textbook style worthy but does not read like one. Whether a user yourself, a loved one of a user, or a worker in some type of rehab, you will find this a valuable resource. The writer gives God all the glory for his long-lasting recovery.

As a Co-Founder of Teen Challenge this story is a personal blessing to me. I highly recommend it.

ENDORSEMENT by Cardwell C. Nuckols, Ph.D.

Dr. Rawson Carlin **A RENAISSANCE MAN.** *"I would probably be dead or in prison if I did not discover the true joy of serving God."* The darkness becomes a beacon of Light as Dr. Carlin describes his spiritual life journey. Many don't seem to acknowledge struggles, trials and tribulations pave the road to transformation.

WE SUFFER TO GET WELL

WE SURRENDER TO WIN

WE DIE TO LIVE

WE GIVE IT AWAY TO KEEP IT

"Based on my experience, alcohol and drugs are facsimiles for being filled with the Holy Spirit." Dr. Carlin's thoughts align with those to Carl Jung, "His craving for alcohol as the equivalent, on a low level, of the spiritual thirst of our being for wholeness, expressed in medieval language: the union with God." Alcohol and drugs are the right direction, just the wrong method. The spiritual approach gets both the direction and the methodology absolutely as it should be.

The author writes of an enlightened approach to healing. He speaks from lessons learned in living life to its fullest, whether in pursuit of recklessness and dereliction or Christ-consciousness. By merging traditional wisdom (Self Help, changing People, Places and Things) with the esoteric nature of the Spirit (contemplation, meditation, forgiveness, the Supernatural, etc.) and good works allows one to regain in recovery something lost…and to move well beyond this point secondary to immediate divine intervention and/or the more common "educational" variety occurring over time.

Dr. Carlin is an honorable man, a Light upon this world and a missionary to those in need. His story, his style, and his learned conclusions make for a very captivating reading and learning experience. It has been a privilege to read and learn from his work.

"May the God of peace make you whole and holy, may you be kept safe in body, heart and mind, and thus ready for the presence. God has called you and will not fail you." I Thessalonians 5:23-24

Cardwell C. Nuckols, Ph.D., An internationally recognized expert in clinical and spiritual recovery from addictions. Dr. Nuckols' passion and mission are to assist in the integration of emerging scientific research with traditional spiritual and self-help knowledge.

Endorsement of **Greater than a Higher Power** *by* **Karl Benzio, MD**

Rawson's fast-paced, never-stop, energizer bunny life was initially fueled and misdirected by hurt. But since tapping into the much Highest Power, Jesus Christ, his positive, grateful, hope-filled servant heart is clear fruit of his transformation. And so is the lasting healing he's led many others to. As a Christian psychiatrist, I've seen theologians and clinicians argue about whether addiction is a sin, disease, or psychological defect while the poor addict is neglected, improperly treated, and dies. But I am so happy to see Rawson's easy-to-read, often humorous unpacking of addiction's spiritual element shows both science and faith are important, with Christian faith generating the power and guiding principles we need while psychiatric science equips us to steward our mind so we can apply this power and principles and be actual doers of the word.

Once we become doers of the word, that is, consistent Godly decision-makers, God's amazing tool of neuroplasticity rewires, or renews, our diseased or reprobate mind for not just meager recovery, but an abundant life through profound PsychoSpiritual healing. To me, this is Practical NeuroTheology.

Rawson blends what he's learned as a scientific clinician with the redemptive power of God he's experienced as a sinner saved by grace to share spiritual nuggets and application steps you can use today to access this amazing healing and achieve your God-given potential, just as Rawson did.

So if you want to be healed, sit back, strap in, and get ready for Rawson to use his down-home demeanor to make an overwhelming case that the God of the Bible is the Highest Power, then he will introduce you plain and simple to Him so He will set you free!

Karl Benzio, MD, is a Board Certified Psychiatrist, Co-Founder and Medical Director of Honey Lake Clinic, and Founder of Lighthouse Network.

Why Should You Read This Book?

You will discover how the so-called natural recovery from addictions is often actually due to supernatural recovery. This book teaches you specific methods to follow to overcome addiction through Jesus Christ, the highest power in the universe. The strategies presented will change your life by showing you the techniques and processes that will help you become totally free from addiction. You will learn what the Bible says about alcohol and drugs, passages of which most people are not aware. You will be inspired by the author's personal story of life situations and struggles and how he got free from alcohol, drugs, and criminal behavior. The goal is to infuse you with hope for yourself or anyone battling addiction.

About the Author

Dr. Carlin is president of E Care Counseling, PLLC in Mooresville, North Carolina, where he has a private counseling practice. He has personally overcome alcohol and drug abuse and has been instrumental in helping thousands of people find freedom from addictions. He lives in North Carolina with his wife, youngest son, and toy poodle dog. His oldest son and grandson live in Findlay, Ohio. He and his family enjoy short mission trips to foreign countries. He has worked in the addiction treatment field for more than 25 years in both secular and Christian faith-based programs. He has earned a bachelor's degree in Social Service, two post-graduate degrees – in Pastoral Psychology and Counseling and Master of Divinity – and a doctorate in Ministry. Plus, he is a Licensed Clinical Addictions Specialist, Master Addictions Counselor, Certified Clinical Supervisor, Licensed Clinical Mental Health Counselor Supervisor, National Certified Counselor, Board Certified-Tele Mental Health Provider, North Carolina Problem Gambling Provider, and an ordained minister of the gospel who has pastored churches.

TABLE OF CONTENTS

INTRODUCTION
GREATER THAN A HIGHER POWER

I s there really a higher power that trumps all other known higher powers in recovery from addiction? If so, is it too politically incorrect to talk or write about? Although there are numerous models and theories of treatment interventions for recovery from alcohol and drug use disorders that have their merits, I believe that I have discovered and experienced a power higher than all others that sets people totally free from addictions. What you may not realize is how the belief in something greater than all other higher powers has been successfully breaking the bondage of addiction for centuries. It is available to all who believe and are willing to commit themselves to the principles in the Bible that can release the power of God Almighty through Jesus Christ and the Holy Spirit.

Miracles of deliverance from many forms of addictions are available now. You can break free from any addiction to alcohol and drugs, gambling, rage, shopping, depression, sex, pornography, anxiety, the internet, etc. The problem is that many do not know the real supernatural power available today to free them or how to access it. I reveal what the Bible says about drug addiction in the pages of this book, plus share principles for overcoming addiction.

I had an alcohol and drug abuse problem that I could not shake loose. I tried to quit many times to no avail. I will share my story and the principles that I learned and that have totally transformed my life. You too can experience the freedom and joy of an addiction-free life without negative side effects. Since graduating in 1969 from Teen Challenge Training Center in Rehrersburg, Pennsylvania, a Christian faith-based residential therapeutic program, I have never had a slip or a relapse with alcohol or drugs.

I have worked in the addiction treatment field for more than 25 years in both secular and Christian faith-based programs. I have earned a bachelor's degree in Social Service, two post-graduate degrees – in Pastoral Psychology and Counseling and Master of Divinity – and a doctorate in Ministry. Plus, I am a Licensed Clinical Addictions Specialist, Master Addictions Counselor, Certified Clinical Supervisor, Licensed Clinical Mental Health Counselor Supervisor, National Certified Counselor, Board Certified TeleMental Health Provider, North Carolina Problem Gambling Provider, and an ordained minister of the gospel. I have also pastored churches.

I have shared on numerous television and radio stations my expertise in overcoming addiction. I have taught continuing education courses for addiction and mental health therapists for years via webinars and conferences in the U.S.A. and other countries. I want you, as a reader, to know that I have extensive experience in treating addictions and mental health disorders. I believe that I understand both the addiction treatment field and theology. I want to share the key insights so that others can experience victory in their journeys to recovery.

My intention in this book is not to explain or to find fault with secular models or theories of addiction treatment intervention because many books and studies have already been published about them. There are many pathways to recovery that have produced varying results. I share numerous Biblical truths, research findings, and testimonies, plus personal autobiographical experiences that will add insights to my thesis.

I also provide reasoning regarding who I believe is the highest power and how to experience ongoing victory over the pull of addictions. Numerous studies that I highlight in this book confirm that the majority of people overcome alcohol and drug addictions without treatment. They "mature out" or experience natural recovery, which, I believe, is, in most cases, a supernatural recovery.

Many people in the world are addicted to something. Addictions come in many forms and can bring down just about anyone; no matter your social/economic, race, or gender—addiction is around us. Most people know a family member, a friend, or an acquaintance struggling with an addiction. You might not even realize that you are currently suffering from addiction right now. Addiction is a real problem today that has a devastating negative impact affecting millions around the world. Many people are in denial, or they romance their addiction without really understanding it or how to release themselves from its clutches. My hope is that when you finish this book that you will know how to overcome addiction for yourself, a family member, or a friend by following the principles that I share.

CHAPTER ONE

MY STORY

My parents tried to raise me right, but somehow at about 11 years old, I picked up a bad attitude and began fighting and getting into trouble. I started smoking cigarettes, fighting, and getting my thrills from delinquent behavior, like skipping school, giving teachers and other authority figures a hard time, throwing things at cars, and breaking windows. My rebellious attitude led to a cycle of getting high or drunk, making dumb decisions, and then getting arrested or endangering the lives of others. Looking back, it is hard to believe I survived to adulthood, let alone until the age of 19 when I finally turned my life around.

I was born in 1950 in Findlay, Ohio, where I was raised as the third of six sons. My father served as an army lieutenant in both World War Two and Korea. He was an attorney and the mayor of Findlay for eight years. My mother was Miss Richmond, Virginia at one point. She was introduced to Jesus Christ by a friend, Helen McCartney, and became deeply committed to her faith and raising six boys. We attended services on Sunday morning, Sunday night, and Wednesday night, plus Sunday School classes, revival meetings, and vacation Bible schools. My mother required my brothers and me to have family devotions with her every morning before we left for school. She was very sincere about serving God and sharing the good news of the Gospel with others. She seemed to spend hours daily, praying and studying the scriptures. She became an evangelist, and she also traveled to preach the Word of God.

I probably prayed to receive Jesus Christ into my heart about a dozen times, but I backslid in about a month each time because I thought that I was missing out on the fun and the pleasures of this world. I wanted to go to Heaven and avoid Hell, but I thought living for God was boring because you could not drink smoke, jump rope, or "do the hoochie-coochie."

Meanwhile, my father usually attended another church on Sunday mornings, so my brothers and I could choose to go with him or to my mother's church. He was a good man that spent most Saturdays with his sons, but he had an alcohol problem himself. On mornings after my father was out drinking, I would sneak into his bedroom and steal money from his pants pockets. That was just the beginning of my shenanigans.

Overall, my early childhood was full of activities. Since we had a big backyard, many neighborhood friends played football and Wiffle ball at our house, and basketball and baseball in nearby fields and courts. My brother Scott was one year ahead of me in school and my brother Dan was one year behind me in school. While in junior high school, my brothers Scott, Dan, and I competed to see who could do the most sit-ups and push ups, and climb a rope faster than others on annual fitness tests. All three of us almost always won the fitness categories for our grade levels. Even as adults, for more than 25 years, when the Carlin brothers got together, we often had push up contests. Scott and Dan have won trophies in ping pong. We had a ping pong table in our home and all the Carlin brothers were very good ping pong players. We have often played ping pong competitively during some of our reunions. Both Scott and Dan have won ping pong tournaments, and Dan has won billiard championships. My brothers and I belonged to the YMCA and often spent time playing ping pong, basketball, or swimming. My mother encouraged all her sons to learn to play the piano or guitar. All my brothers learned to play an instrument but me. I can only play the radio and blow a shofar.

All my brothers seemed quite talented, and I never thought I was not as good as them in many things. My oldest brother, Bill, sang in musical performances and acted on stage, and he traveled playing music in rock bands. Scott was gifted in sports, especially basketball in high school where he was all-state—one of the best five in Ohio. He had many college basketball scholarship offers and went to a college in Kansas. Dan pole-vaulted and played basketball in junior high and he sang in a rock band. My late brother Bob was some kind of chess master and played in numerous tournaments. My brother John is a great guitar player and singer. I tried pole-vaulting and could not get the hang of it. I played basketball in junior high but was third string and mostly sat on the bench during games. In hindsight, I realize that I was better than most in basketball because I at least made the teams, while dozens of others got cut or did not make the team.

Somehow, I felt that I did not measure up to my brothers and became the rebellious tough guy that got into a lot of trouble. When I was about nine years old I began shadowboxing daily in front of a full-length mirror. This process probably contributed to me getting into many physical fights as I grew older. I got some attention, but it was mostly negative. At birth, I weighed more than 10 pounds and had wide shoulders, so my father called me Buffalo Muscles. Later, my nickname became Buff. Despite my behavior at times, my brothers and I usually got along and would always stick up for one another. Today, we all live in different states across America, but we love each other and keep in touch and all meet for reunions periodically. I am glad that I overcame my inferiority, and now realize that I have some skills in helping people. But back in Findlay in the 1960s, that lesson was yet to come.

Our family home was two blocks from Donnell Junior High School and the stadium where high school football games were played. I used to have supplies of tickets from previous events and sold them, depending on the color of the ticket needed. With the help of a friend, we bent bars in a spot on the fence that surrounded the stadium to sneak in and out. During football games, friends and I often threw tomatoes and eggs into the stands. We also put night crawlers and other yucky things on seats of parked cars for a laugh. Soon, my tricks went from mischievous to something far worse.

During high school, I do not remember ever doing any homework assignments. I attended summer school after 10th grade because I flunked so many classes. Somehow, I did graduate from high school in 1968, despite habitual drugs and alcohol abuse. I got into many fights and enjoyed beating up bullies and challenging authority figures. Throughout my time attending Findlay High school, students were not allowed after lunch to go back into the building where the classrooms were until a bell rang. A student hall monitor, usually a big football player, would guard the main door to prevent students from entering. However, I would just walk right in. A few times, a hall monitor would try to stop me, but I told him that I would knock him out in front of everyone, so he would just quiet down and sit back. After that, I never stopped going wherever I wanted to go. No hall monitors ever stood up to me or told the principal, as far as I remember. I had a chip on my shoulder and took pride in being tough.

The downside of having a reputation as a tough guy is that other tough guys challenged me at times. I started hanging out with many older guys that had been incarcerated or in trouble with the law. Clearly, I was rebellious. During high school, there was a rule that you had to have your shirts tucked in and wear socks. I never met those elements of the dress code, even in the freezing winter. I cannot remember anyone ever confronting me about the way I dressed. Several people told me that I walked like I was looking for a fight. I was in good physical shape and purposely allowed people to hit me in the stomach, barely flinching because my stomach muscles were strong. I used to sleep through many classes and no teacher dared to confront me. My father and I were called into the principal's office for a meeting and I defied them both. My father was very disappointed in me.

People used to rake piles of leaves onto the curb in front of their homes and I would set them on fire as I rode by on my bicycle. For a while, my brother Dan and I would throw a dummy in front of a car for excitement. I cannot remember if we got in trouble for that. One time, a police car was left parked and running in the parking lot of the Teen Center. So, I got in and drove it about two blocks away and parked it. I never got caught for that. Friends and I used to throw mud on cars driving on Main Street until one of the friends got caught and told on the rest of us. Of course, my father was notified again.

My friends and I hung out after hours at a friend's parents' bowling alley, bar, or golf course where they worked. We drank alcohol, smoked cigarettes, took drugs, bowled games, drove around on golf carts, and ate food. A couple of my friends had horses and I enjoyed riding them. The caretaker at the stables occasionally gave us moonshine to drink. We also hung out at friend's houses when their parents were out of town. I usually made sure that no one trashed the places and we cleaned up the house before we left. My friends and I were having fun, so why would I want to change my life at this point? However, things changed, and I started to generate negative consequences because of my lifestyle. I used to go swimming at a quarry or pond outside of town with one of my brothers and a couple of friends. Out on a country road, we put a cherry bomb in a random mailbox and drove away. A couple of minutes later, the sheriff himself pulled us over because we blew up his mailbox.

My brother Dan and I often snuck out at night by climbing out a second-story window. Climbing back into the house was a challenge, especially if we were intoxicated. I used to steal chocolate milk that was left outside of the school cafeteria early in the mornings. I also broke into the school often to play on the basketball court with my friends. At age 15, I got into an argument with my father over a haircut and left home. I hung out with some older guys and got drunk, abused drugs, broke into places, and stole things. My father found me about a month later, living in a mobile home with a 21-year-old and an 18-year-old friend. He asked me to come home. I was drunk and refused. He told me that I could live in an apartment that our family owned if I promised to finish high school.

For a while, I would sleep in the county jail and walk to school and back. Sometimes one of my brothers snuck and gave me rides to Findlay Senior High School. At least once, a sheriff's deputy picked me up after school and took me to get evaluated by a psychologist or psychiatrist. No one ever told me the results of these evaluations. I escaped briefly from the county jail once when my father and a brother came to visit. I ran out the front door and Scott chased after me. He convinced me to go back to jail immediately, and I did.

Some of my friends and I stayed out all night drinking and drugging at a park. The next morning, we were at a restaurant where a couple of the employees confronted me in the restroom about us leaving a mess. The sheriff came in person, rather than sending a deputy. He told me that I would have to go in front of the juvenile court judge. I replied that I would rather shoot the judge than go to court. So, I got arrested for making a terroristic threat. A judge from another county had to come in and preside over the court session. On the day of the hearing, the sheriff personally handcuffed me and walked me from the jail to the courthouse. After 15 minutes, the judge ordered the sheriff to personally take me to get my haircut so that not one hair was more than an inch long. I stood up and told the sheriff and the judge in foul language where to go. Again, my father, who was an attorney, was shocked and disappointed in me. That day, I was labeled incorrigible and sentenced to a month at the Juvenile Diagnostic Center in Columbus, Ohio, then six months at an Ohio Youth Commission reformatory followed by parole. I still have a letter that I wrote to my mother from the reformatory, telling her that I was going to change and be a better person. However, I did not have the willpower to make major changes as needed. Therefore, I continued my rebellious lifestyle.

I was treated briefly with medication for a sexually transmitted disease. When some of my friends found out, they would clap their hands in the school hallways each time they saw me. It did not bother me at all. I was sexually active, and my oldest son was born just after I turned 18. My behavior was erratic, inspiring a couple of parents to take out restraining orders to keep me away from their daughters. At that age, I did not care what they or any other authority figure said.

Several times, when I got pulled over by a police officer, they knew who I was, but when they asked my name, I would say Donald Duck or Mickey Mouse. One policeman used to hassle me while my

9

friends and I hung out at the parking lot of Ohio Oil or Marathon Oil Company. I called him a Barney Fife (after the character from *Andy of Mayberry*) and called him a wimp and worse. Later, two police cars pulled up in front of my apartment building on Main Street and a sergeant called me over. He told me that the police officer that I called Barney Fife wanted to box me in a match at the YMCA. Cocky and 18, I told the sergeant that I would be glad to do it. I had been boxing for years and would love the chance to knock him out, I said. However, many police officers came to watch, which was fine with me if I could have just as many of *my* friends there, I added. I was looking forward to that match, but never heard anything more about it after that.

My friends and I enjoyed living on the edge of life. We used to take turns riding fast on the hood of cars on country roads or bumper skiing in the winter for thrills. We did some unofficial drag racing down Main street and on country roads. We used to jump off high cliffs at a quarry and try different drugs for the adventure. I remember partying with members of a motorcycle club and drinking booze from a "righteous boot." A biker took off a boot in which we poured in alcohol, ashes, cigarette butts, hot sauce, and whatever else we could think of. Then we passed it around and drank from it. We did a lot of crazy things like "shooting the moon" at school buses. We were wild and enjoyed it.

One night, I literally shot myself in the face. I had a small tear-gas gun and tried to shoot it outside a few times, but it would not fire. Then I walked into my apartment and told a friend that the gun did not work so I pointed it at myself under my nose over my top lip. I pulled the trigger and BOOM—it went off. I ended up visiting the emergency room and being questioned by the police. I looked like Adolf Hitler for a while with a dark black scab for a mustache.

To keep up the pace, I was always hustling for money for food or to buy alcohol and drugs. I bought a box of empty capsules at a drug store and filled them with baking soda powder and sold them as a Spanish fly aphrodisiac at high school. I never had anyone come back to tell me it was fake stuff. Once a friend told me that it was reported on the radio that someone was selling the stuff at the high school, I quit. After that, I worked part-time for a carpet and cleaning company and cleaned the local drivers' license office once in the evening. I saw a stack of blank driver's licenses on a desk and took about 100 of them from the bottom. Back then, the driver's licenses were paper only and your information was typed on them. I sold the blanks so that teens could fill out their own so they could buy beer or get into a bar to drink. My father heard about it and asked me about the driver's licenses, so I flushed the remaining ones down the toilet.

Another time, three guys showed up at a house where I was staying with an older friend, and they asked me to sell them some marijuana. I did not have any at the time, but I told them to come back in a couple of hours. I went to a grocery store and bought a jar of dill weed, put some in envelopes, and sold it to them. A few days later, they came back for more, and I did the same thing. I was alone when I answered the door and thought I would have to fight them because it was not real weed that I sold them previously. But they never had a clue that I had deceived them.

I became adept at scamming people to get what I wanted. My waitress girlfriend would give me her paycheck and tips. I used to call in orders at a certain fast-food restaurant and pick the food up at the drive-in window without paying. An employee, who I had called beforehand to order, always took care of me. I used to steal cigarettes, steaks, and other food daily from a grocery store near my apartment. I never, ever got caught. At night, I would steal watermelons left outside in front of the grocery store. Often, when in another town, I would sit down in a restaurant and order a meal, then walk out without paying. My friends and I used to pick some corn from cornfields and cook them outside on an open fire so we could eat. I was the lookout guy for a friend that broke into a gas station and robbed a safe, but we never got caught.

I really disliked bullies picking on others, and I enjoyed beating them up. However, I quickly realized that I could make money from the situation. I had guys tell me that a bully was going to beat him up if they did not pay him money. Instead, I got paid to protect them by confronting the bullies. Then I realized that I could make money by talking to some bullies so they would threaten guys, who would pay me to protect them; I then split the money with the bullies.

Soon, there was nothing I would not do for a buck or a thrill. Because my best friend was older and wild, he would eat things like dead bird guts or bugs while I took bets from teens that did not think that he would do it. I also collected money from teens to pay for alcohol that my older friend would buy. Of course, I kept a cut for our personal alcohol, drugs, food, or gas money. I siphoned gasoline from other vehicles regularly and somehow never got caught. I have walked out of stores with cases of beer while a friend distracted the cashier. I needed new tires on my car, so a friend stole a brand-new set of tires from a gas station. At night, my friends and I would drive up beside a fence at a power company and steal heavy rolls of copper wire that were the size of car tires. Then we would burn them to make them look old and sell the copper.

You get the picture—I was a hustler and thief. I did what I could to survive financially, including selling drugs. I share this information not to brag about my misconduct, but to inform you of the risky things people can do to obtain alcohol and drugs. Also, I want to let you know that with God's help, anyone can change through the highest power of all. Thank God that after I really surrendered my life to Christ, I quit doing those terrible things. I have regrets for many of the things I did, but I know that I am forgiven and now live my life to help others overcome their addictions too. At one point a few friends and I counted 100 guys that we knew from our hometown of about 38,000 that had been sent to prison. No matter what anyone has done or is doing to support an addiction, anyone can have a better life without addictive behavior through Jesus Christ.

CHAPTER TWO
WHAT IS ADDICTION?

There are many different definitions of what addiction is. According to the latest Diagnostic and Statistical Disorder Manual of Mental Disorders (DSM-5), Substance-Related and Addictive Disorders only include substance use and gambling disorders. Therefore, gambling disorder is the sole condition in a new category of behavioral addictions. Other potential addictions (internet, exercise, shopping, etc.) are not included due to "insufficient peer-reviewed evidence to establish the diagnostic criteria and course descriptions." However, many believe that addictions to food, sex, pornography, self-harm, and other conditions should also be considered behavioral addictions. Some of the predominant models and/or theories of addiction are presented briefly in this chapter. The way that addiction is defined usually influences the model or method of treating it. There are many paths to recovery from addiction.

According to the Merriam-Webster Dictionary, addiction is defined as 1) a compulsive, chronic, physiological or psychological need for a habit-forming substance, behavior, or activity having harmful physical, psychological, or social effects and typically causing well-defined symptoms (such as anxiety, irritability, tremors, or nausea) upon withdrawal or abstinence: the state of being addicted, and 2) a strong inclination to do, use, or indulge in something repeatedly.

As a teenager, partying consumed my life; I drank alcohol, sniffed toluene (a chemical in paint thinners), and used drugs, including marijuana, hashish, cocaine, Demerol, morphine, opium, amphetamines, and LSD. One of my friend's mother was a nurse and we used to look up pills in her Physicians' Desk Reference to help us know what medications would get us high. A former medic in Vietnam brought home large trunks of morphine and other drugs for us to use.

Sometimes we had "salad bowl parties" where all types of pills were put into a bowl and you would take a handful. Once, after taking a big handful of drugs with uppers, downers, and all-arounders, I did both number one and number two in my pants. When I was 17, three older friends and I hitchhiked to Mexico and California to experience the hippie life of free love and drugs. We had fun, but we were terrible hippies since the four of us liked to fight and were not fully into peace. One friend got busted and spent five years in prison in California and another one was incarcerated in county jail. I phoned home to Ohio and found out that my father was dying of cancer, so I hitchhiked back home. I was 18 years old, drinking beer in a bar when a friend told me that my father died in a VA hospital. I smashed the glass front door of the bar with my hand as I left, and I still have scars on my right hand. Anger became a bigger and bigger part of my life. I kept going in and out of jail for different offenses, mostly for assault and battery.

Why would someone choose to live this way? Let us look at some of the scientific theories that align with my life story.

Addiction as a Disease

Since 1997, the U.S. National Institute on Drug Abuse has advocated a brain disease model of addiction. The National Institute of Drug Abuse (NIDA) defines addiction as a chronic, relapsing brain disease that is characterized by compulsive drug-seeking and use despite harmful consequences. When a disease is chronic, that means it is long-lasting. It cannot be cured, but it can be managed with treatment. Respected institutions like the American Medical

Association and the American Society of Addiction Medicine define addiction as a disease. Studies published in top-tier publications like *The New England Journal of Medicine* support the position that addiction is a brain disease. A disease is a condition that changes the way an organ functions. Addiction does this to the brain, changing this vital part of you on a physiological level. It literally alters the way the brain works, rewiring its fundamental structure. That is why scientists say addiction is a disease.

Others think addiction cannot be a disease because it is caused by the individual's choice to use substances. The choice does not determine whether something is a disease. A disease is what happens in the body because of those choices. Others argue that addiction is not a disease because some people with addictions get better without treatment, usually after hitting the bottom or experiencing a serious family, social, occupational, physical, or spiritual crisis.

Marc Lewis, a psychologist and former addict himself, is the author of *The Biology of Desire: Why Addiction is Not a Disease*.[1] Lewis's argument is actually fairly simple: the disease theory, and the science sometimes used to support it, fail to take into account the plasticity of the human brain. Of course, "the brain changes with addiction," he writes. "But the way it changes has to do with learning and development—not disease." The problem is, there is a lot of vested interest – and financial investment – in perpetuating the disease model. He believes that if someone thinks their addiction is an incurable illness that they are going to have to live with, they may lose the incentive to overcome it. Therefore, the disease model is an obstacle to healing.

Dr. Lance Dodes reported that "Addiction has very little in common with diseases. It is a group of behaviors, not an illness on its own. It cannot be explained by any disease process. Perhaps worst of all, calling addiction a "disease" interferes with exploring

---

[1] The Biology of Desire: Why Addiction Is Not a Disease by Marc Lewis, July 14, 2015 by Public Affairs ISBN 1610394372 (ISBN13: 9781610394376)

or accepting new understandings of the nature of addiction."[2]

Many clinicians disagree with the position that addiction is a disease. Tim Holden reported that "Addiction does not meet the criteria specified for a core disease entity, namely the presence of a primary measurable deviation from the physiologic or anatomical norm."[3] Labeling addiction as a disease suggests that the brain can no longer change; that it's an end state. But no, it's not an end state. We know that treatment isn't required by most to overcome addiction, so, in that sense, it's not a disease. And the changes in the brain that occur because of addiction are not irreversible.

I believe that millions of people in the world are deceived by drugs and alcohol. People begin using alcohol and drugs for different reasons, and some of them become addicted. Their addiction can change them to do things that they never thought they would do, such as lie, cheat, steal, and engage in immorality. This ultimately leads to financial problems, social relationship issues, marriage breakups, legal problems, unstable employment, etc. They become deceived into having thoughts that produce negative addictive behaviors, which in turn affects their whole lives and impacts those close to them. Families and employment productivity become damaged. The world is greatly affected by deception due to the influence of drugs and alcohol on societies. Big pharmaceutical companies have provided many life-saving drugs. However, some of them have deceived due to greed and have profited from questionable tactics that have resulted in thousands and thousands of people becoming addicted to opiates.

Biopsychosocial theory of addiction

The bio-psycho-social model of addiction is an attempt to explain how addiction occurs and is maintained. It is meant to give

---

[2] Lance Dodes M.D. Is Addiction Really a Disease? Psychology Today posted Dec. 17, 2011. https://www.psychologytoday.com/us/experts/lance-dodes-md
[3] Tim Holden, MMed (Psych), Psychiatrist and assistant professor CMAJ. 2012 Apr 3; 184(6): 679. doi: 10.1503/cmaj.112-2033

a framework of understanding so that treatment can be more effective. It posits that biological/genetic, psychological, and sociocultural factors contribute to substance use and all must be taken into consideration in prevention and treatment efforts.

Personally, I believe in a bio-psycho-social-spiritual model of addiction that takes into account biological, psychological, social, and spiritual factors. Medical clinicians evaluate biological factors, while mental health clinicians assess psychological and social functioning, and clergy or spiritually trained clinicians address spiritual conditions. Therefore, a holistic approach is utilized to treat addicts. The Greek word "pneuma", for the Spirit, and also the Greek words "logos" for the general word of God and "rhema" for a specific revelation word from God, would be applied along with the biopsychosocial aspects.

Dr. Karl Benzio, a psychiatrist and medical director at Honey Lake Clinic in Florida, spoke in a workshop at the NAADAC conference in Washington, DC in 2012 on the subject of "Is Addiction Sin, Disease, or a Psychological Defect?" At the end of his session, he reported that addiction is all three, and he gave sound reasoning for his conclusion. I attended the workshop and liked his presentation and his conclusion.

The Twelve Steps of Alcoholics Anonymous

The famous 12 steps of Alcoholics Anonymous indicate the importance of believing in a power greater than ourselves. The references range from God as we understand Him, admitting to God, asking God to remove our shortcomings, prayer, and meditation to improve our conscious contact with God as we understand Him, praying only for knowledge of His will for us and the power to carry that out. AA and other 12-step groups, such as Narcotics Anonymous and Gamblers Anonymous, hold these truths. Active participation in 12-step meetings includes really working the steps and working closely with a sponsor. The program adopts the slogan "Works if you work it" to reinforce how progress arises from living these practices. We:

1. Admitted we were powerless over alcohol—that our lives had become unmanageable.

2. Came to believe that a Power greater than ourselves could restore us to sanity.

3. Made a decision to turn our will and our lives over to the care of God *as we understood Him.*

4. Made a searching and fearless moral inventory of ourselves.

5. Admitted to God, to ourselves, and to another human being the exact nature of our wrongs.

6. Were entirely ready to have God remove all these defects of character.

7. Humbly asked Him to remove our shortcomings.

8. Made a list of all persons we had harmed and became willing to make amends to them all.

9. Made direct amends to such people wherever possible, except when to do so would injure them or others.

10. Continued to take personal inventory and, when we were wrong, promptly admitted it.

11. Sought through prayer and meditation to improve our conscious contact with God *as we understood Him*, praying only for knowledge of His will for us and the power to carry that out.

12. Having had a spiritual awakening as the result of these steps, tried to carry this message to alcoholics and to practice these principles in all our affairs.[4]

Personally, I have participated in numerous 12-step groups, but have not continued my participation. Why? Because I have been

---

[4] https://www.alcohol.org/alcoholics-anonymous/ Used with permission.

highly active with my personal relationship with God and in Christian activities that have empowered me. Others choose to actively maintain participation in 12 steps for decades and benefit greatly from it. These programs – such as Alcoholics Anonymous, Narcotics Anonymous, and Gamblers Anonymous – have been instrumental in helping addicts all over the world. Plus, many of the participants believe in Jesus Christ as their higher power. I encourage clients to embrace 12-step meetings to help them find a steady footing.

Celebrate Recovery is a Christian faith-based program that has been very successful using its own 12 steps:

Celebrate Recovery 12 Steps and Biblical Comparisons

1. We admitted we were powerless over our addictions and compulsive behaviors; that our lives had become unmanageable. I know that nothing good lives in me, that is, in my sinful nature. For I have the desire to do what is good, but I cannot carry it out. Romans 7:18 NIV

2. We came to believe that a power greater than ourselves could restore us to sanity. For it is God who works in you to will and to act according to his good purpose. Philippians 2:13 NIV

3. We made a decision to turn our lives and our wills over to the care of God. Therefore, I urge you, brothers, in view of God's mercy, to offer your bodies as living sacrifices, holy and pleasing to God, which is your spiritual act of worship. Romans 12:1 NIV

4. We made a searching and fearless moral inventory of ourselves. Let us examine our ways and test them and let us return to the Lord. Lamentations 3:40 NIV

5. We admitted to God, to ourselves, and to another human

being the exact nature of our wrongs. Therefore, confess your sins to each other and pray for each other so that you may be healed. James 5:16a NIV

6. We were entirely ready to have God remove all these defects of character. Humble yourselves before the Lord, and he will lift you up. James 4:10 NIV

7. We humbly asked Him to remove all our shortcomings. If we confess our sins, he is faithful and will forgive us our sins and purify us from all unrighteousness. 1 John 1:9 NIV

8. We made a list of all persons we had harmed and became willing to make amends to them all. Do to others as you would have them do to you. Luke 6:31 NIV

9. We made direct amends to such people whenever possible, except when to do so would injure them or others. Therefore, if you are offering your gift at the altar and there remember that your brother has something against you, leave your gift there in front of the altar. First go and be reconciled to your brother; then come and offer your gift. Matthew 5:23-24 NIV

10. We continue to take personal inventory and, when we were wrong, promptly admitted it. So, if you think you are standing firm, be careful that you don't fall! 1 Corinthians 10:12

11. We sought through prayer and meditation to improve our conscious contact with God, praying only for knowledge of His will for us, and power to carry that out. Let the word of Christ dwell in you richly. Colossians 3:16a NIV

12. Having had a spiritual experience as the result of these steps, we try to carry this message to others and practice these principles in all our affairs. Brothers, if someone is caught in a sin, you who are spiritual should restore them gently. But watch yourself, or you also may be tempted. Galatians 6:1

NIV[5]

I also encourage people to consider incorporating belief in the Trinity (God the Father, Jesus Christ the Son, and the Holy Spirit) as their higher power.

What the Bible says about Alcohol and Drugs

Unless you know what to look for, drug use in the Bible isn't always evident. The word "drug" is not found in the Bible, but that does not mean that it is not referred to in its texts. Since many Hebrew and Greek words are translated differently in some Bible versions, you may not readily find scriptural references. I took Hebrew and Greek classes in seminary and learned how to find the meaning of words in both the old and new testaments. Therefore, "sorceries" basically means drugs, so drugs actually are mentioned in the Bible, but just by different names. Here is an example: Revelation 18:23, "All the nations were deceived by your sorcery [Gk. pharmakeia]."

Vine's Expository Dictionary says the word "Sorcery (PHARMAKEIA) English, (pharmacy, etc.) primarily signified the use of medicine, drugs, spells; then, poisoning; then, sorcery." Galatians 5:20, Revelations 9:21, and 18:23 cite φαρμακεία (pharmakeia) as "sorcery, craft, black magic." Our modern words of "pharmacy" and "pharmaceutical" are derived from the Greek pharmakeia, Strong's Exhaustive Concordance #5331. Pharmakeía means the occult, sorcery, witchcraft, illicit pharmaceuticals, trance, magical incantation with drugs." (Gal. 5:20; Rev. 9:21; 18:23; Sept.: Ex. 7:22; Is. 47:9, 12) Pharmakeia refers to "the use of magic, often involving drugs and the casting of spells upon people—'to practice magic, to cast spells upon, to engage in sorcery, magic, sorcery.'"

Galatians 5:19-20 reads, "Now the deeds of the flesh are evident, which are: immorality, impurity, sensuality, 20 idolatry, sorcery [Gk. pharmakeia], enmities, strife, jealousy, outbursts of anger, disputes, dissensions, factions." It seems to me that the deeds

---

[5] https://www.celebraterecovery.com/resources/cr-tools/12steps

of the flesh referred to in Galatians are often part of the behaviors associated with people addicted to alcohol and drugs.

Sorcery often includes the practice of using unbiblical means to foretell the future, summon spirits, cast spells, etc. Sorcerers are supposedly possessors of supernatural powers from an evil source. Meanwhile, Jesus Christ possesses supernatural powers that are good and more powerful than any sorcerer. There were many instances of real or pretend sorcery among the Jews in Biblical days, which seems to have been designed by Satan and wicked men to bring into disrepute the miracles of Christ and his apostles. I believe that there are people today that have been unwittingly influenced by evil spirits to disrepute the great power of Christ manifested through anointed believers. Therefore, many minds are poisoned to disbelieve the good news of the gospel and the power of God today. As a result, the ministry in Jesus' name is dismissed as unreal, which influences people to not call upon the Lord for freedom from their addictions. In the New King James Version in Acts 13:8, "Elymas the sorcerer (magician) withstood them [Barnabas and Saul], seeking to turn the proconsul away from the faith." In other words, Elymas tried to influence the Roman official representing the consul not to believe in Jesus.

Strong's Exhaustive Concordance indicates that the Old Testament Hebrew word reference 3784 kashaph means to practice sorcery or use witchcraft. A primitive root properly is to whisper a spell, for example, to enchant or practice. Therefore, drug use is also mentioned in the Old Testament. The Old Testament contains many references to drug use or drug users (sorcery – pharmakeia) and since the Hebrew scriptures were translated into Greek (the Septuagint) in the 3rd century BC they are easier to discover with research. The Septuagint, a Greek version of the Hebrew Bible (or Old Testament), including the Apocrypha, made for Greek-speaking Jews in Egypt, was adopted by the early Christian churches and includes witchcraft and sorcery as involving drugs.

The word "witch" occurs twice in the King James Version, namely, (1) in Exodus 22:18, "Thou shalt not suffer a witch (the Revised Version, British and American, "a sorceress") to live"; (2)

in Deuteronomy 18:10, "or a witch" (the Revised Version, British and American, "or a sorcerer"). The Hebrew word is in both cases the participle of the verb (kishsheph), denoting "to practice the magical article and drug enchantments." We can recognize that sorcery and witchcraft are much the same. Witchcraft is defined as the mixing of potions. Drugs and potions have traditionally been used in witchcraft to induce deeper subconscious states which can enable persons to have fellowship and communication with evil spirits. What we need to understand is that, throughout history, people who used sorcery were also involved in drugs. That's why in the Bible where the words "sorcerer" or "sorcery" are used, we are looking at drug use as well. Remember, all nations are deceived by drugs as if they are under a spell.

There are a number of scriptures that speak about drinking alcohol in the Bible, although it is not condemned. However, drunkenness is repeatedly brought up in the Bible as being unacceptable. Both in the Old Testament and the New Testament, drinking alcohol is allowed, but it is preferred for people to be sober-minded.

Ephesians 5:18 states, "Do not be drunk with wine, in which is dissipation; but be filled with the Spirit." We can replace alcohol with drugs, and, in most cases, the meaning remains primarily the same. Most addiction therapists believe that alcohol is also a drug. The Apostle Paul could certainly have said that addiction leads to debauchery. This scripture also points out that being drunk (or addicted) is counter to being filled with the Holy Spirit.

In Proverbs 20:1, "Wine is a mocker; intoxicating drink arouses brawling, and whoever is led astray by it is not wise." This could be taken as alcohol can cause a drunk to say horrible things and fight. Substance abuse certainly makes a person do things they wouldn't usually do, such as lie, say hurtful things, become sexually promiscuous, neglect occupational or family duties, etc.

Proverbs contrasts drinking with being wise. Abusing substances is certainly not a wise thing to do. We know that Jesus turned water into wine and he most likely drank it too. However, on the cross, he refused wine mixed with a drug to ease his suffering. Mark 15: 22-23a says, "And they brought Him to the place Golgotha (which is translated, place of a skull). Then they gave Him wine mingled with myrrh to drink, but He did not take it." Mixing alcohol with some prescription and illicit drugs can be very dangerous.

Stimulant Use Disorder Diagnostic Criteria

A checklist like this one helps to assess a possible Stimulant Use Disorder as described in DSM-5. It determines a pattern of amphetamine-type substance, cocaine, or other stimulant use leading to clinically significant impairment or distress, as manifested by at least two of the following occurring within a 12-month period.[6]

Criteria for Stimulant Use Disorder
1. The stimulant is often taken in larger amounts or over a longer period than was intended.
2. There is a persistent desire or unsuccessful efforts to cut down or control stimulant use.
3. A great deal of time is spent in activities necessary to obtain the stimulant, use the stimulant, or recover from its effects.
4. There are cravings, a strong desire, or an urge to use the substance.
5. Recurrent stimulant use results in failure to fulfill major role obligations at work, school, or home.

---

[6] Reprinted with permission from the Diagnostic and Statistical Manual of Mental Disorders, Fifth Edition, (Copyright 2013). American Psychiatric Association.

6. There is continued stimulant use despite having persistent or recurrent social or interpersonal problems caused or exacerbated by the effects of the stimulant.

7. Important social, occupational, or recreational activities are given up or reduced because of stimulant use.

8. There is recurrent stimulant use in situations in which it is physically hazardous.

9. Stimulate use is continued despite knowledge of having a persistent or recurrent physical or psychological problem that is likely to have been caused or exacerbated by the stimulant.

10. Tolerance, as defined by either of the following:

a. A need for markedly increased amounts of the stimulant to achieve intoxication or desired effect.

b. A markedly diminished effect with continued use of same amount of the stimulant.

Note: This criterion is not considered to be met for those taking stimulant medication solely under appropriate medical supervision, such as medications for attention-deficit/hyperactivity disorder or narcolepsy.

11. Withdrawal, as manifested by either of the following:

a. The characteristic withdrawal syndrome for the stimulant (refer to Criteria A and B of the criteria set for stimulant withdrawal, p. 569).

b. The stimulant (or a closely related substance) is taken to relieve or avoid withdrawal symptoms.

Note: This criterion is not considered to be met for those taking stimulant medications solely under appropriate medical supervision, such as medication for attention-deficit/hyperactivity disorder or narcolepsy.

Note: In 2013, the American Psychological Association updated the DSM, replacing the categories of *substance abuse* and *substance dependence* with a single category: *substance use disorder,* with three sub classifications—mild, moderate, and severe. The symptoms associated with a substance use disorder fall into four major groupings: impaired control, social impairment, risky use, and pharmacological criteria (i.e., tolerance and withdrawal). Reprinted with permission from the Diagnostic and Statistical Manual of Mental Disorders, Fifth Edition, (Copyright 2013). American Psychiatric Association.

Since the Bible presents the ability to produce magic spells by sorcery and witchcraft using drugs, it appears that each of the 11 DSM-5 diagnostic criteria could be attributed to a drug-induced spell just as much as to a disease or other theories. It sounds different, but is it a possibility? Often drug and alcohol use is fueled by something that largely contributes to addictive behavior.

Trauma and addiction

Often people self-medicate with alcohol, drugs, sex, food, gambling, or other compulsive behaviors to cope with trauma and emotional pain, to numb the hurt with quick temporary relief. The link between trauma-related disorders and substance use disorders has been empirically established. When I do assessments with clients, I usually asked them if they can think of anything that could be fueling their addiction. Most clients can identify some trauma—suffering from an abusive past or emotional turmoil that contributed to their addiction. I have had grown men crying in my office while telling me their deepest secret for the first time—that they had been sexually abused as a child. The term "dry drunk" has been used by some in Alcoholics Anonymous to describe alcoholics who have quit drinking but were frustrated in sobriety because they have not dealt with negative emotions or trauma issues.

Many families have some level of dysfunction. In the past 10 years, I have been almost shocked to hear that some alcoholics and drug addicts started by using it with a parent. Some people have low self-esteem because they have been told repeatedly that they are stupid, worthless, or should have never been born. Some develop shame. We all have done things that we feel guilty about due to the mistakes we have made. Shame is not merely thinking you made a mistake. Shame is thinking and feeling that you *are* a mistake.

Trauma-related memories and emotional pain can unconsciously or consciously feed addictive behavior. In Luke 4:18, Jesus said that He has been sent to "heal the brokenhearted." Isaiah 61:7 states, "Instead of your shame you shall have double honor; instead of confusion, they shall rejoice in their portion. Therefore, in their land they shall possess double; everlasting joy shall be theirs." It is important to identify and address trauma, shame, and other negative emotions that affect thinking and behavior. For many years, addiction-treatment programs solely addressed alcohol and drug problems while mental health professionals, for the most part, did not treat addiction. However, now co-occurring substance use disorders and mental health disorders are treated together in an integrated manner.

Our past childhood experiences can affect our lives for good or bad, depending on our response. When I was about three years old, my father came home with a new car. I think it was a black Cadillac. On our first ride with the whole family, I was sitting on the back passenger-side seat of a four-door car and could not close the door. I was holding it while trying to get my father's attention, but he apparently did not hear me over my loud brothers. When were got about 100 feet from our house, I fell out onto the street. Surprisingly, I only received a few scrapes or bruises. However, I vowed in my heart that I would always listen to anyone crying out for help and help them. Perhaps that is why I defended people that were being bullied. That experience probably planted inside me the seed for future ministry and counseling.

On the negative side, I often felt inferior to my talented brothers and probably acted out in bad ways to get attention. However, there was something far more sinister lurking inside me that I had yet to identify and release.

CHAPTER THREE
DEMONS

C ould some addictions be influenced by demons? The expression that some people struggle with their demons is commonly used today to refer to mental and emotional problems. Probably most people in America and the world do not believe in the reality of demonic activity today. Some Christians have read accounts of demonic activity in the Bible and believe that evil spirits may have been active in Biblical days thousands of years ago but have somehow disappeared from Earth. Some believe that there might be some demons in Africa, but not in America.

While other Christians acknowledge that demons may be real, they avoid thinking or discussing the subject. My understanding of evil spirits comes from the Bible and life experiences. For instance, King Saul in the Old Testament was troubled by an evil spirit and was relieved temporarily when David played music for him. My understanding of the Greek word for demonized in the New Testament means that people, whether possessed or oppressed, were influenced to do evil and bizarre things.

I have not shared this very often, but I was possessed by demons and was delivered from them in 1969. At the time, I was facing the possibility of going to prison for five years for crimes. I had been abusing alcohol and drugs while living a rebellious life full of physical fights and criminal activities. I hung out with a rough crowd and was in and out of the city and county jails in my hometown numerous times.

However, I had a praying mother who played a key role in my salvation, as you will soon see.

After leaving home after that fight with my father over a haircut, he agreed to let me live in a family-owned apartment on Main Street if I stayed in high school until graduation. Even a year after he died, I continued to live there and partied with my friends. The building was across the street from the Hancock County Court House and a half a block from the Findlay Police Department. We knew that the cops did not like us due to our criminal behavior and suspected drug dealing.

I used LSD with my friends and had many great trips on it. I loved it at the time. However, one night after dropping a couple of tabs of LSD, we drove into the countryside around 1 am. to smoke marijuana, out of sight of the police. Everything was going well as about five of us smoked up in a car. Then we got out and stood in a circle in a cornfield, giggling and saying things like "Wow, this is cool, far out, and this is it." Then something strange happened to me. Suddenly I saw horns appear and disappear intermittently on the heads of my friends.

I started thinking, "This is it, the end of the world. Jesus Christ must have come back for the Christian believers and I was stuck on Earth with demons." I told my friends what I was experiencing, and they said, "Just maintain, Buff. Everything will be cool. It is just a trip." I remember when we got back into the car, my heart was pounding from fear. I said, "Take me home to my mother's house." They knew that I did not live there and tried to talk me out of it. But I insisted, so they dropped me off at her house. I kept thinking: my mother is a good Christian and if she is still on Earth then the Rapture of Christians had not taken place. I just had to know.

So, at about 2 am. I woke my mother up. I remember going into her bedroom and hugging her. "Are you really my mom?" I asked her. Then I looked at her and she grew horns that also appeared and disappeared sporadically. I was freaking out. My mother started praying and pleading the blood of Jesus. I got up and walked around the house in confusion and fear. Eventually, I crashed and fell asleep on a sofa in the living room.

When I woke up the next day, my mother said "Buff, do not take drugs or the Devil will get you." I was so shaken up that I decided there would be no more LSD for me. I was not concerned about the other illicit drugs I was taking, including marijuana, hashish, cocaine, morphine, opium, or various forms of speed.

I managed to stay away from acid for a couple of weeks out of fear. Then I went with a couple of friends to Columbus, Ohio to buy some drugs. Somehow, after scoring the drugs we ended up without a ride and had to hitchhike. My two friends both dropped some acid and invited me to take some, but I refused. In the back of my mind, I was afraid that the Devil would get me if I used LSD again. I wrestled with thoughts of the Devil getting me and decided it was just a bad trip. My next trip will be great, I told myself, just like they used to be. After an hour or two, I decided to take another hit of acid.

My trip was going okay at first, despite the fearful thoughts in the back of my head. We ended up at a party where I stood in front of a stove, grooving on the colors that I saw in the heat waves arising as it warmed the apartment. Then, someone that I had never met before tapped me on the shoulder. When I turned around, he said "Remember that bad guy that your mother told you about and you wouldn't listen?" Then he grabbed my neck with both hands, like he was going to choke me, and said, "I am the Devil." I freaked out and started beating on him. Someone took him away, perhaps to a hospital.

Everywhere I looked, I saw devils in people's faces and floating around the room. My best friend Nick tried to calm me down. He suggested that I think about my girlfriend or something else. When I looked at Nick, his face looked like the Devil with the intermittent horns. I kicked him in the face. As he wiped the blood from his mouth, he said, "Buff, you are my best friend, and I don't want to hurt you" and went outside. Nick was older and bigger than me and had boxed in Golden Gloves tournaments. I am forever grateful that he chose not to fight me.

I ended up in the back of a car with two "acid heads" from my hometown, who I barely knew. They informed me that they were taking me to my apartment. However, I thought that they were demons taking me to throw me in "The Pit." From the back seat, I punched and kicked them. They were probably afraid of me and did not try to hit back. Fortunately, we did not have an accident.

When we reached the back alley behind my apartment building, I saw my brother Dan and a couple of friends rolling a drunk for his billfold. I watched weird shapes and colors moving on the back of the building. Somehow, even in my frightened state, I was relieved to see my brother. For some reason, his face is the only one that did not look like a demon or devil. Dan tried to comfort me. He was probably high on something himself. I remember that I was afraid to use the bathroom unless Dan stayed with me. I keep telling myself that, if this were just a trip and I woke up tomorrow okay and not in Hell, I would set things right with God.

The next day I received and read some gospel tracts in the mail from my mother. I kept thinking, "I need to get right with God." I was so relieved that the world and my life had not ended with me going to Hell. I knew by then that the guy that had tapped me on the shoulder the night before was just someone playing mind games as people do, such as making noises like a bomb is falling and then exploding. He probably had no idea about the conversation that I had with my mother a couple of weeks prior to that. However, even though I rationally knew that it was all just a bad trip, I also knew that I was not right with God. I wanted to avoid going to Hell or being influenced by demons. My mother phoned that day and informed me that a pastor and a group of people were fasting and praying for me to be delivered from satanic influences. She asked me to go to the pastor's home that night for prayer.

Although I was seriously considering giving my life to the Lord, something held me back from consenting to go. My mother kept calling me daily until the third day, when I agreed to go to the pastor's home for prayer. I did not tell any of my friends where I was going. After all, I was a tough guy, and they would not have understood.

When I arrived, the pastor, the assistant pastor, and a bank president were waiting for me. They asked me some questions then laid their hands on my head and shoulders and began praying. I am not sure how long the session took. I remember thinking, "What have I gotten myself into? I need to get out of here." While they were praying and rebuking the Devil, I felt something evil leave my body and heard the deliverance team praising God.

However, I felt something else evil in me. I literally barked and growled. I knew that something evil was still in me and I wanted it out. I shocked myself when I firmly said, "Devil, I command you to leave me in the name of the Father, the Son, and the Holy Ghost." I felt it leave and immediately began praising God and raising my hands in worship. Although I felt weird or different, I felt a deep sense of being clean and much loved before God. I repented for my sins and accepted Jesus Christ into my life. It felt better than any drug high that I have ever experienced. We all praised the Lord for a while then they gave me hugs and some instructions to maintain living in victory.

After my exorcism experience, I started witnessing to my friends about turning my life over to Jesus. They listened and basically said, "That's cool if that is what you want to do." I still hung out with the same friends and in my old haunts. I told people in bars about giving my life to Jesus. Most were shocked or surprised because I had been so mean, wild, and crazy. My belief system probably influenced my LSD trips and the demons that I saw under the influence.

For 50 years now, I have occasionally prayed for dozens of people that have been delivered from demonic influences. Whether these people were possessed or oppressed, I have seen lives transformed after deliverance encounters. I do not look for demons under every rock or think that most mental health, behavioral problems, addictions, or life-controlling problems are due to demonic activity. I have only participated in an exorcism about once per year. However, if I perceive that someone is demonized, I am willing and able to set the person free through the power and authority that I have through Jesus Christ. I genuinely believe that some people suffering from these problems could only be saved through faith in Jesus Christ by believers who are willing to fulfill the portion of the Great Commission of casting out devils.

Believers can overpower evil supernatural forces

The Roman Catholic Church practices exorcisms when needed and so do many Pentecostal and Charismatic Christians all over the world. There is a network of deliverance churches in America that practice exorcism. The fact that many people – including Christians, non-believers, medical doctors, and mental health providers – are not familiar with this practice or think it too strange does not mean that it is not a real phenomenon. If the secular world and most Christians would set aside preconceived mindsets and take time to study and consider demonic deliverance as a viable option practiced with positive results by some, it would open the door to greater dialogue between the sacred and secular. You do not have to understand exactly how something works to recognize its value. Christians that practice exorcisms at times understand that what they have been doing has brought great relief to people. Yet, most mental health and addiction therapist providers dismiss it as hocus pocus. Contrary to Hollywood portrayals of exorcisms in movies that seem to emphasize that demonic forces are more powerful than priests and Christian believers, God anoints believers with the authority here on Earth with power that is more powerful than all evil supernatural forces.

Two passages of scripture record are referred to as the Great Commission. Matthew 28:16-20 states, "Then the eleven disciples went away into Galilee, to the mountain which Jesus had appointed for them. When they saw Him, they worshiped Him; but some doubted. And Jesus came and spoke to them, saying, 'All authority has been given to Me in heaven and on earth. Go therefore and make disciples of all the nations, baptizing them in the name of the Father and of the Son and of the Holy Spirit, teaching them to observe all things that I have commanded you; and lo, I am with you always, even to the end of the age.'" According to Mark 16: 14-20, "Later Jesus appeared to the eleven as they sat at the table, and He rebuked their unbelief and hardness of heart because they did not believe those who had seen Him after He had risen. And He said to them, 'Go into all the world and preach the gospel to every creature. He who believes and is baptized will be saved, but he who does not believe will be condemned. And these signs will follow those who believe: In My name, they will cast out demons; they will speak with new tongues; they will take up serpents; and if they drink anything deadly, it will by no means hurt them; they will lay hands on the sick, and they will recover.' So then, after the Lord had spoken to them, He was received up into heaven and sat down at the right hand of God. And they went out and preached everywhere, the Lord working with them and confirming the word through the accompanying signs."

Some disciples doubted Jesus when he lived on Earth, having "unbelief and hardness of heart." Today, many still doubt that believers have the authority to cast out demons. Can we all agree that some people with addiction and mental health disorders have exhausted almost all attempts of various treatments without success? In the process of practicing medicine, some medical doctors go through a process of ruling out diseases and sometimes they get stumped on what is causing some symptoms. Perhaps, some patients have conditions that are beyond scientific knowledge or medical training that could be addressed successfully spiritually by the exorcism of evils spirits by believers.

In Mark 9:17-29, the Apostles, even using the authority given to them, were not able to cast out a demon from a possessed boy. Jesus had to do the exorcism personally. He criticized the lack of faith and explained that some evil spirits could only come out through prayer and fasting.

In Acts 19:13-17, the seven Jewish sons of Sceva tried to exorcise a man in the name of Jesus, who was preached by the Apostle Paul. To their disappointment, the possessed man jumped onto them, giving them such a beating that they left the place naked and bleeding. Only genuine believers filled with the Holy Spirit have the authority to command evil spirits or demons to leave in the name of Jesus.

Ephesians 6:12 says, "For we wrestle not against flesh and blood, but against principalities, against powers, against the rulers of the darkness of this age, against spiritual hosts of wickedness in the heavenly places." However, Jesus Christ is higher than all other powers and will give us complete victory in we call upon Him and allow Him to work in our lives. This spiritual warfare is one to which the masses of Earth's inhabitants are totally oblivious. But Heaven and Hell, demons and angels are real, and I am compelled to reveal to you the nature of Christ as I have come to know Him. I hope and pray that you will become a believer and recognize your need for salvation.

In the Great Commission that Jesus gave to the church recorded in the Gospel of Mark 16:15-20, he said, "These signs shall follow them that believe; In my name shall they cast out demons…they shall lay hands on the sick, and they shall recover." And they did go and cast out devils. Verse 20 reports, "And they went forth and preached everywhere, the Lord working with them, and confirming the word with signs following." About 25 percent of the people that Jesus healed, as recorded in the four Gospels, were demonized. Jesus cast out devils as part of the healing process for some. In Luke 8: 26-39, Jesus encountered a man who had had many demons for a long time; he wore no clothes, lived in tombs, cried out with a loud voice, and broke chains. Jesus cast the devils out of the man then the demons begged Jesus to let them go into a herd of pigs, who subsequently rushed down the steep bank into the lake and drowned. As a result, the man sat at the feet of Jesus now clothed and in his right mind. As a result of his encounter with Jesus Christ, this man was healed.

Years ago, I sat in a college class led by a Licensed Professional Counselor and Licensed Addictions Therapist. My professor reported that very man was probably a schizophrenic who needed mental health treatment, but he was not plagued by demons or evil spirits. I spoke up and asked, "If that wasn't demons, then why did the herd of pigs violently jump off a cliff and drown? And how did the man break the chains that bound him?"

"The story portrays mental illness and the references to demons are figurative and not literal," the professor responded.

I held my tongue because I realized that the professor had a mindset that was contrary to my beliefs and experiences. He is a good man with a Ph. D. in counseling that probably has preconceived ideas that prevent him from accepting or considering the Biblical reality of being demonized in the past or the present. But I knew my own truth was undeniable.

CHAPTER FOUR
TEEN CHALLENGE PROGRAMS

David Wilkerson, a small-town pastor from Pennsylvania, read a story in LIFE magazine in 1958 about several New York City teenagers on trial for a gang-related murder. His heart was stirred so much that he traveled to New York and tried to speak at their trial. A newspaper took a picture of Rev. Wilkerson holding up his Bible. He preached the good news of God's love to addicts and gang members on the streets of tough neighborhoods. He and his brother, Don, founded Teen Challenge Ministries in Brooklyn in 1959 by opening the first Teen Challenge program to help addicts in a residential center. Now there are Teen Challenge programs across the world. In my opinion, it is the most effective of all drug and alcohol programs that are based on the love of Christ and Biblical truths to assist addicts to become free from addiction.

Rev. Wilkerson, along with John Sherrill, co-authored the bestselling book *The Cross and the Switchblade* in 1963, which tells about his early days in New York. The book was made into a motion picture in 1970, starring Pat Boone as Rev. Wilkerson and Erik Estrada as gang leader Nicky Cruz. Rev. Wilkerson was instrumental in helping thousands of addicts to get free from their addictions. After he died in an automobile accident, he left a legacy of love and hope. I have had the privilege of meeting him and his brothers Don and Jerry. The family has dedicated themselves to the ministry of Teen Challenge.

Rev. David Wilkerson founded Teen Challenge on the premise that being a "born again" Christian will overpower the need for drugs. The program's mission statement is simple: Teen Challenge is Christian people helping men and women with life-controlling problems of drug and alcohol addiction, to transform their lives through a relationship with Jesus Christ so that they become productive members of society. Teen Challenge consists of Christian faith-based residential therapeutic communities that provide a loving environment that is spiritually rich with hope. The staff is sincere, seasoned ministers, former addicts, and support people that serve as role models for the residents, who are referred to as students. The staff provides encouragement, discipleship, mentoring, and prayer. [7]

The Wilkerson brothers opened the first Teen Challenge program in Brooklyn in 1959. Currently, there are more than 200 Teen Challenge centers in the U.S.A. and more than 1,400 centers in 125 nations. I believe it is the largest program for overcoming substance use disorders in the world. There are numerous other similar Christian faith-based programs around the world. However, many people are unaware of Teen Challenge's existence. Its basic philosophy can be cited as: "We believe that sincere faith in Christ is the motivation needed to extract the deep-rooted symptoms that cause dependence on drugs." We ask each addict to fill the void in his or her life with dynamic self-motivation of the Gospel. The overall encompassing philosophy is that God will help you with any or all problems.

My Exposure to Teen Challenge

I took drugs a few times after the exorcism and talked to my pastor about my struggles. He recommended that I go into the Teen

---

[7] Excerpt taken from U.S. Government survey entitled, "RESEARCH SUMMATION – H.E.W. 1976 Study on Teen Challenge Training Center, Rehrersburg, PA, by Catherine B. Hess M.D., MPH., National Institute of Drug Abuse.

Challenge program in Pennsylvania to get away from my environment and get discipled in the faith. Rev. Delmar Ross had come to the Hancock County Fair with some students from the Teen Challenge Training Center in Pennsylvania about a year earlier and witnessed to me and my friends about Christ. At that time, I was not ready to really listen. My mother had previously sent me *The Cross and the Switchblade,* which I read in jail, so I was aware of the genesis of Teen Challenge.

When I was ready, I took the bus to Pennsylvania where Rev. Ross, the superintendent of the program, picked me up and drove me to the Center. He remembered meeting me at the Fair and I told him that I had surrendered my life to Jesus about six weeks prior. I threw my last pack of cigarettes in a wastebasket at the bus station because I knew that smoking was not permitted at Teen Challenge. We arrived at the beginning of a chapel service and Rev. Ross asked if I wanted to say anything in the chapel. "I came here to see if God is real; if not, I will leave," I replied. Although I had recently been born again, I still had some doubts. However, I promised my mother that I would stay at least six months. That way, I would sincerely give God time to reveal Himself to me more and convince me that He loved me and had hope and a future for me. Each morning when I woke up to face my three roommates who had been heroin addicts, I told myself, "I am at Teen Challenge and I am here to learn and grow in Christ." Fitting into the program was not difficult. I committed to submitting to authority figures and obeying the rules.

I attended chapel and three Bible study classes daily, plus I worked three hours on weekdays on the farm at Teen Challenge. I got baptized in water and filled with the Holy Spirit while growing in Christ. Rev. Ross took me to many schools and churches to share my testimony. Rev. Frank Reynolds, executive director of the program, drove me to a television station that taped me presenting two 30-second public-service messages to discourage drug abuse; they were aired throughout Pennsylvania in 1969. I sang in a choir at Teen Challenge and we recorded an album entitled "From the Heart of God's Mountain." I gave my testimony a couple of times at youth rallies where Rev. Wilkerson preached and legendary Christian songwriter Dallas Holm sang. Many youths received

Christ into their hearts at those rallies. I usually spent a couple of hours daily on my knees, praying in the prayer room. Although I loved sports, I did not participate in any games at Teen Challenge. I desperately desired to have an intimate relationship with Christ and gave myself fully to seeking the Lord with all my heart.

Despite my devotion, I struggled with fears that I would revert to my former lifestyle. I sincerely prayed for God's wisdom, encouragement, and direction. A few months into the program I read this passage in Philippians 1:6: "being confident of this very thing, that He who has begun a good work in you will complete it until the day of Jesus Christ." I received a revelation from that Scripture that transformed my thinking. I cried tears of joy and knew deep inside me that from that moment, I would never backslide. *I have never had a slip or relapse to alcohol, drugs, or criminal activity in 50 years.* Soon afterward I read Jude 24: "Now to Him who is able to keep you from stumbling (falling), and to present you faultless before the presence of His glory with exceeding joy."

In John 8:31-32, Jesus said, "If you abide in My word, you are My disciples indeed. And you shall know the truth, and the truth shall make you free." The truth is that Jesus Christ can save or deliver everyone from addiction.

In 1975, the National Institute of Drug Abuse conducted a research project and found that 86 percent of those who complete the Teen Challenge program remained drug-free. In 1994, the University of Tennessee conducted another study and also found that Teen Challenge had phenomenal success. Research completed in June 1999, supervised by Northwestern University in Illinois, once again showed that 86 percent of those who completed the Teen Challenge program had stayed free of drugs.[8] The study took three

---

[8] Northwestern University, The Teen Challenge Drug Treatment Program in Comparative Perspective, A Dissertation Submitted to the Graduate School in Partial Fulfillment of the Requirements For the Degree, Doctor of Philosophy, Field of Political Science by Aaron Todd Bicknese, Evanston, Illinois, June 1999, page 118.

years. They interviewed graduates from the East Coast to the West Coast. They found that Teen Challenge graduates were "more likely to be living normal lives holding down jobs and not needing further treatment."[9] They found that "nearly all have escaped the 'revolving door phenomenon' of substance abuse treatment."[10]

They also found that 84 percent of graduates attend church weekly.[11] The researchers said that two of the most powerful features of Teen Challenge are the work training and strict discipline.[12] The research compared Teen Challenge to other drug programs, and of the other group, only 41 percent were employed one and two years later, while 90 percent of the Teen Challenge graduates were employed one and two years later.[13] They found that the students in the program have an attitude of "It is a privilege to be here" and were very thankful for the chance they had to participate in the Teen Challenge program.[14] The interviewer said that the Teen Challenge graduates seem to describe their experience at Teen Challenge as something revolutionary. When asked why they no longer use drugs, the Teen Challenge graduates said that "Jesus Christ filled a void in their life."[15]

These studies regarding the successful outcomes or results of Teen Challenge graduates demonstrate that "The Jesus Factor" works greater than secular programs and even Alcoholics

---

[9] The Teen Challenge Drug Treatment Program in Comparative Perspective, page 222.

[10] The Teen Challenge Drug Treatment Program in Comparative Perspective, page 229.

[11] The Teen Challenge Drug Treatment Program in Comparative Perspective, page 228.

[12] The Teen Challenge Drug Treatment Program in Comparative Perspective, page 240.

[13] The Teen Challenge Drug Treatment Program in Comparative Perspective, p.172, 229 & 232)

[14] The Teen Challenge Drug Treatment Program in Comparative Perspective, page 235.

[15] The Teen Challenge Drug Treatment Program in Comparative Perspective, page 222.

Anonymous or other Twelve Step programs. The Twelve Steps help many people overcome addictions. However, to them God is described with the phrase "as we understand Him." This is probably the only spiritual program in the world in which you can invent your own God any way you like. Jesus Christ is higher than any higher power of man's invention as "understood" by many. According to Teen Challenge graduates, the nature of the commitment to Jesus Christ is crucial. It is not enough to have a vague belief in a higher power; one must commit to the Christ of the Bible. Teen Challenge has been a major positive influence on my life that has helped me understand Jesus Christ and the abundant life He offers to those who are willing to believe and accept Him as their personal Savior and Lord. The "Jesus Factor" in my opinion is the best way to overcome addiction.

Relapse and Recovery

Many addiction treatment and programs have low success rates or do not track their success rates. Dr. Thomas McLellan is the founder of the Treatment Research Institute, an independent, nonprofit research and development organization dedicated to science-driven reform of treatment and policy in substance use, and a professor of psychiatry at the University of Pennsylvania. He has more than 35 years of experience in addiction treatment research. I attended workshops in Cheyenne, Wyoming in 2004 in which he presented training on the Addiction Severity Index and American Society of Addiction Medicine Criteria. He asked the approximately 150 attendees to raise their hands and report the success rate of their treatment programs and no one raised a hand. I remember him reporting that he has spoken to thousands of clinicians across America while doing those training that treats addictions for more than 20 years and has asked this question and no one had ever raised their hand to answer. It makes you wonder how effective addiction treatment is. Hopefully, treatment outcomes are being tracked better now.

Relapse seems to be expected as normal in secular treatment and recovery literature. Substance dependence is generally referred to as a chronic relapsing disease. However, that concept seems foreign to me because I spent many years working for Teen Challenge programs that were Christ-centered and had a high success rate. Therefore, when I started working in the secular substance abuse treatment and recovery arena, I repeatedly read or heard that chemical dependency relapse was the norm.

While working as an addiction therapist for the Department of Veterans Affairs in Wyoming, some veterans completed inpatient treatment at one of the VA Medical Centers, then participated in outpatient substance abuse treatment with me at a VA Community Based Outpatient Clinic. Often, these veterans expressed their concern that being taught – even before their release from inpatient treatment – they would probably relapse, gave them feelings of despair and hopelessness. Telling clients in treatment that statistically they will probably relapse several times can be very discouraging. Yes, some people in recovery do fall back to their old habits. Yet, I found and still believe that relapse is rare in people that have truly given their lives to Jesus Christ and remain active in spiritual activities. I don't think that we should bury our heads in the sand and deny that some people do regress. However, in my experience, speaking about relapse with doom and gloom with clients in treatment can create a sort of a self-fulfilling prophecy. It seems wiser to me to offer hope and encouragement so that clients can believe and expect that they indeed will recover from their addictions.

Years ago, I did addiction recovery work through a federal grant called Access to Recovery in Casper, Wyoming. I visited a 16-year-old young man in a juvenile detention facility. He informed me that he had been in a substance abuse treatment group in which the addiction therapist informed the group that 80 or 90 percent of them would relapse back to alcohol and drug abuse and commit more crimes. The young man told me that he stood to his feet and asked to be excused from the group because he wondered "what was the use of being in a group when the therapist believes that I will not change?" He was not allowed to leave and remained for weeks, mentally turned off or tuned out. How much benefit was received from the program led by a therapist that did not believe that the participants would make positive changes in their lives? Maybe the narrative needs to change to offer hope.

The importance of developing a positive rapport or therapeutic alliance has been well documented. If the therapist or counselor believes that their clients will inevitably relapse and be unsuccessful in their recovery efforts, this often comes across consciously or unconsciously to clients. It makes a big difference when a therapist trusts in you more than the power of addiction. If the therapist believes that you are not going to recover, how can they wholeheartedly provide encouragement, hope, and positive support that will breed a transformed life?

In the early 1980s, I was the executive director of Teen Challenge of Louisiana, with three facilities including a residential therapeutic community with 40 males. One of the students returned to the facility after a weekend pass and admitted that he had used cocaine. According to the program rules, I could have kicked him out of the program or given him various other sanctions. However, when I met with him I listened to him to gather the facts and circumstances about his cocaine use. He was 25 and had grown up in a housing project in New Orleans. I asked about possible triggers, preplanning, peer pressure, etc. I pleasantly surprised him by telling him that I believed in him and agreed to allow him to stay in the program. I told him to take his next pass and to call me if he needed encouragement, and I would drive to see and support him. I told him I believed that he would not use cocaine again and would await his return so he could tell me about his success. He came back from his next pass with a big smile on his face. He hugged me and cried tears of gratitude. He said no one ever had told him that they believed in him before. Actually, I cried a few tears of joy, because he did not use cocaine again and started to believe in himself. I reinforced how I cared about him and that Jesus loved him. When he graduated from the program, I hired him, and he became a great asset to our staff and clients in the program. Later, he completed two years of Bible college and has never relapsed back to cocaine or any other drug. I am pleased with the dramatic changes that he has made in his life. What would have happened to him if I had kicked him out of the program? I don't even like to think about that scenario.

Around 2004, a presenter at a training workshop for addiction professionals talked about the importance of having collateral information, including criminal background checks. The presenter asked, "When is an addict or alcoholic lying?" To answer his own question, he said, "Whenever they open their mouths." The presenter reported that substance abusers always lie, especially about their past criminal histories. Many of the 30 attendees agreed with the speaker.

This bothered me, so I spoke up. I shared how years earlier I applied for a counseling job in New Orleans and probably was denied employment because a criminal background check reported that I had spent 30 days in the Toledo Workhouse in Ohio for assault and battery. This information was not true. Yes, I had been convicted for assault and battery and had spent time in the Hancock County Jail, but never at the Toledo Workhouse. A friend of mine was convicted with me and he served time in Toledo. Apparently, a court clerk mistyped the information. If it happened to me, couldn't it happen to others also?

I also shared general information about a veteran that I was working with. His criminal background check by a probation officer during a presentencing investigation erroneously reported that he had raped a woman in a state that he had never been in. Fortunately, the veteran had a good attorney that checked into the matter and proved that the report was incorrect. After I shared the two situations, the presenter reported that criminal background checks are very rarely wrong and still insisted that substance abuse clients always lie. I thought to myself that this professional, and many others in the field, have negative mindsets that definitely affect the way they relate to clients. Perhaps they are burned out and have little faith left for their clients.

Yes, I know that some clients lie, but let us not paint them all with the same brush. Sure, clients have lied to me, but I have not become cynical toward them and do not treat them with disdain. Probably most addiction therapists that do both assessments and treatment would be more effective if they demonstrated some positive vibes toward their clients. Yes, I am familiar with denial, rationalization, minimization, and other excuses addicts are often armed with as psychological defense mechanisms. They need to be challenged appropriately and dealt with. However, in our modern times of cultural awareness and sensitivity, it seems that therapists would build a better rapport if they believed that addicts tell the truth sometimes. An addict can probably sense if they are being judged and disregarded. How can they have faith in therapy if the therapist does not believe they are capable of telling the truth, are manipulative, and most likely are not going to change?

Being culturally sensitive should include faith issues also. When I was 16 years old in a reformatory, I was told to report to the chaplain's office. The first thing that he said to me was "What the hell brings you here?" I immediately tuned him out due to my Pentecostal Christian upbringing, which instilled within me the belief that true Christians do not use that kind of language. I was not living my faith and certainly used bad language myself, but I had strong beliefs about how Christians should speak. Right or wrong in my thinking at the time, I did not respect that chaplain as a man of God and would not listen to anything that he tried to tell me after that first impression. I was required to attend chapel services on Sundays, but I did not listen to anything that chaplain might have had to say about God and the principles to live by that could have benefited me. My mindset, and perhaps the insensitivity of the chaplain, resulted in a waste of time for me. The chaplain may have read the information that identified me as having a Pentecostal background. Perhaps he was trying to be "cool or hip" with me or was trying to relate to me on some kind of streetwise level. I know many chaplains that would never use that approach.

Years later, I graduated from seminary and joined the Ohio Chaplains Association. I preached in correctional institutions across the state of Ohio and was a volunteer chaplain in several jails and correctional institutions. I was also elected and served as the chairman of the Cuyahoga Correctional Chaplains in Cleveland, Ohio. I have always tried to be sensitive to the beliefs and values of others and to show respect. What if all counselors or therapists working with addicts were sensitive to the spiritual beliefs of their patients or clients and found ways to encourage them in their faith?

Unfortunately, some addiction therapists, due to insensitivity, have discounted the faith of clients, which could undermine their recoveries. Many people seem to dismiss the concept of the power of God to set people free from addictions. They have difficulty believing that a personal relationship with Jesus Christ is a viable answer for addictions and other life-controlling problems.

I attended a conference in Colorado on addictive disorders and heard a psychiatrist speak about acupuncture as a viable treatment option. She had resisted trying it due to her scientific education, yet she came to believe that placing needles in specific places in patients' ears helped them quit tobacco and enhanced their treatment outcomes. She became open-minded after much consideration of the facts and changed her beliefs to incorporate a new therapeutic procedure that has proved successful, although she may have risked her professional reputation. Personally, I have never tried acupuncture, but I am open to it as a means of helping people. It does not conflict with my Christian beliefs. It would be great if others without Christian beliefs would be open to the idea that Jesus Christ has the power to set people free from addictions.

Areas of my life that God helped me change at Teen Challenge

My first challenge at Teen Challenge arose when a student offered me a contraband cigarette, which I turned down. Then another student, who often cut in front of me in the cafeteria line, got into my face and challenged me to fight. I knew that I could easily dust him. However, I always pointed up and said that God would fight for me. He probably thought that I was afraid, but I definitely was not. God used him to test my anger and pride. My next challenge was my girlfriend, who I loved, back in Findlay, Ohio. She wrote me letters and I talked to her on the phone a couple of times. In prayer, God impressed upon me the need to break up with her. It was a deeply emotional decision to obey God and let her go, which I did.

I used to be lazy and rarely worked hard, but here the staff assigned us chores for three hours per day on the farm. A staff member took me and five other students to a field and instructed us to pull the weeds between the corn stalks. I worked for about a week, weeding in the hot sun while the others sat watching, not working at all. They hassled me verbally for toiling away. I told them I was working as to the Lord. I never ratted or snitched on them because I never was one to do that. After that, I was assigned to work every day in an air-conditioned office in the mail room. I believe that God honored me for being faithful. I surprised myself and volunteered to pick up hay on some evenings. I was determined to become a better person.

During my first few months after turning my life over to the Lord, I had what I would call demonic attacks. While sleeping, I would sense a strong evil presence and become frightened. I would try to call out to Jesus but could not utter His name due to intense, paralyzing fear. After a few minutes of trying, I would stutter out "J-J-Je-Jesus" and wake up drenched in perspiration. While at Teen Challenge, when I laid down to sleep, I would sense an evil presence standing by my feet; when I looked, I saw a dark mist. I would pray until I fell asleep. The day that I got baptized in the Holy Spirit and went to bed, I again sensed and saw a dark presence. However, I learned 1 John 4:4: "You are of God, little children, and have overcome them, because He who is in you is greater than he who is in the world." So I said, "Devil you can stare at me all night if you want, but you cannot harm me because greater is Jesus and the Holy Spirit within me than you, and I am protected by the precious blood of Jesus." Then I fell asleep peacefully. It happened a few more nights, then ceased. Knowing, speaking, and applying the word of God are powerful tools for victory. Although my experiences may seem weird, I have had dozens of people throughout my life share similar experiences with me, believe it not.

Although I never studied or completed homework assignments in high school, I was motivated and got straight A's in all of my Bible classes at Teen Challenge. I memorized 50 scripture verses on "soul-winning" in the evangelism class. I have led hundreds of people to Christ throughout my life using those verses. I learned that Jesus loves me and that he will never leave or forsake me. I was discipled by the staff, who took the time to mentor me. The choir director, Jack Schell, Dean brother Rainbow, Executive Director Rev. Frank Reynolds, and Rev. Ross and his wife, Phyllis, were great role models and mentors. Reading and studying the Bible has become a way of life. As result, I have grown in wisdom, maintained sobriety, and have discipled many others in the faith. I got baptized in water and filled with the Holy Spirit while at Teen Challenge. I am glad that I followed my mother's advice. Jesus Christ is real, and He has given me an amazing, abundant life. I also developed public speaking skills while in the program. I truly became a new creation in Christ through the positive role modeling of the staff. God miraculously provided for me to go straight from Teen Challenge into Bible college.

Chapter Five
Natural Recovery or Supernatural Recovery?

In the early 1970s, I attended numerous conferences and workshops on chemical dependency and shared my personal testimony of overcoming addictive behaviors. I was often accompanied by former heroin addicts from Teen Challenge programs who also shared how Jesus Christ helped them overcome their addictions. However, my impression was that the clinicians that appeared to listen attentively and kindly seemed to view us as "Bible thumpers." They dismissed what we said as something they were not comfortable in incorporating into their treatment programs.

Since then, I have attended and participated in scores of conferences and workshops on dependencies and am familiar with the prevailing interventions based upon research, prevalent theories, medication-assisted treatments, and promising practices. Many of them have emerged after receiving millions and millions of dollars of financial backing. However, although probably at least 90 percent of all addiction treatment programs acknowledge the importance of spirituality or a higher power as vital to addiction recovery, Jesus Christ or any specific faith-based methods for addressing addiction are rarely mentioned. It appears that different mindsets, personal opinions, lack of spiritual knowledge, political correctness, or biases and prejudices detour many people from accepting or acknowledging that Jesus Christ could be a major solution to addiction. In my opinion, the major source for overcoming addictions has been overlooked, shunned, misunderstood, misinterpreted, and poorly represented.

Perhaps the hearts of many people have grown dull today due to spiritual ignorance. and the answer that can heal addicts is dismissed in search of something else that is compatible with their belief systems or mindsets. I boldly proclaim the benefits of acknowledging and embracing the truth regarding Jesus Christ, who has the supernatural power to set people free. I invite you to open your mind and your heart to new possibilities about a person that has, does, and will continue to transform lives. This is especially important if the world as a whole will be willing to accept the reality of who Christ is and what he does in the lives of those that believe. In the Bible, in Matthew 13:14-15, Jesus quoted from Isaiah 6:9-10: "Hearing you will hear and shall not understand, and seeing you will see and not perceive; for the heart of this people has grown dull, their ears are hard of hearing, and their eyes they have closed, lest they should see with their eyes and hear with their ears, lest they should understand with their heart and turn, so that I should heal them."

The Unknown God

In a way, I feel similar to the experience of the Apostle Paul and his encounter with people in Athens (Acts 17: 16-34). His spirit was stirred when he observed what was happening in the city and he reasoned with the people and preached about Jesus Christ. Some called him a babbler and some reported that he shared strange things when he mentioned the resurrection from the dead. Paul told them that he perceived that they were very religious. He saw an altar with the inscription "TO THE UNKNOWN GOD" and proclaimed God that made the world and everything in it. He added that in Him we live and move and have our being. Some mocked him, but others joined him and believed. Some may consider me today as a babbler, a proclaimer of strange things, and possibly mock me like they did Paul.

What do you believe? II Timothy 3:5 expresses that some people "have a form of godliness but deny its power." Throughout the Old and New Testaments of the Bible, there are multiple recordings of miracles, and the power of God to perform miracles is still available today. Some believe and receive while others deny and do not believe. I, for one, have experienced God's miraculous power and have witnessed the power of God active in many too numerous to count. Please carefully seek the Lord and learn about His power to perform miracles in your life today. According to Romans 10:17, "Faith comes by hearing, and hearing by the word of God." I challenge you to listen to powerful anointed preaching and teaching of the word of God and study the scriptures for yourself.

Many churches seem to present God as a boring, almost disinterested and powerless, being, but if you take the time to seek, you will find ministers of the gospel and churches that proclaim and experience the supernatural power and presence of God Almighty that is very much alive and thriving; that can and will bless you and heal you today. Freedom and healing from all sorts of addictions and mental health disorders are real and available for you, your family, and friends.

Acts 3 records how the apostles Peter and John were used by God through the name of Jesus to heal a crippled man. Next, Acts 4:1-31 relates how Peter and John were put in custody overnight and questioned the next day by religious leaders. They could not deny that a miracle had happened and asked Peter and John, "By what power or by what name have you done this?" Then Peter and John were threatened to not speak at all or teach about Jesus. However, they prayed for boldness and continued.

Just like them, I choose to boldly proclaim Jesus Christ as Lord with the power to heal and deliver people from addictions today. How will alcoholics and addicts know that Jesus Christ can set them free unless believers boldly and lovingly let them know the truth of His grace, salvation, and miraculous healing power?

Here is the full passage so you can get a better sense of the story:

Acts 4:1-31 Now as they spoke to the people, the priests, the captain of the temple, and the Sadducees came upon them,2 being greatly disturbed that they taught the people and preached in Jesus the resurrection from the dead.3 And they laid hands on them, and put them in custody until the next day, for it was already evening. 4 However, many of those who heard the word believed; and the number of the men came to be about five thousand. 5 And it came to pass, on the next day, that their rulers, elders, and scribes,6 as well as Annas the high priest, Caiaphas, John, and Alexander, and as many as were of the family of the high priest, were gathered together at Jerusalem. 7

And when they had set them in the midst, they asked, "By what power or by what name have you done this?"8 Then Peter, filled with the Holy Spirit, said to them, "Rulers of the people and elders of Israel:9 If we this day are judged for a good deed done to a helpless man, by what means he has been made well,10 let it be known to you all, and to all the people of Israel, that by the name of Jesus Christ of Nazareth, whom you crucified, whom God raised from the dead, by Him this man stands here before you whole. 11 This is the 'stone which was rejected by you builders, which has become the chief cornerstone.'12 Nor is there salvation in any other, for there is no other name under heaven given among men by which we must be saved.13

Now when they saw the boldness of Peter and John, and perceived that they were uneducated and untrained men, they marveled. And they realized that they had been with Jesus.14 And seeing the man who had been healed standing with them, they could say nothing against it.15 But when they had commanded them to go aside out of the council, they conferred among themselves, 16 saying, "What shall we do to these men? For, indeed, that a notable miracle has been done through them is evident to all who dwell in Jerusalem, and we cannot deny it. 17 But so that it spreads no further among the people, let us severely threaten them, that from now on they speak to no man in this name." 18

So they called them and commanded them not to speak at all nor teach in the name of Jesus.19 But Peter and John answered and said to them, "Whether it is right in the sight of God to listen to you more than to God, you judge.20 For we cannot but speak the things which we have seen and heard."21 So when they had further threatened them, they let them go, finding no way of punishing them, because of the people, since they all glorified God for what had been done.22 For the man was over forty years old on whom this miracle of healing had been performed.23

And being let go, they went to their own companions and reported all that the chief priests and elders had said to them.24 So when they heard that, they raised their voice to God with one accord and said: "Lord, You are God, who made heaven and earth and the sea, and all that is in them, 25 who by the mouth of Your servant David have said: Why did the nations rage, And the people plot vain things? 26 The kings of the earth took their stand, And the rulers were gathered together against the Lord and against His Christ. 27 For truly against Your holy Servant Jesus, whom You anointed, both Herod and Pontius Pilate, with the Gentiles and the people of Israel, were gathered together 28 to do whatever Your hand and Your purpose determined before to be done.29

Now, Lord, look on their threats, and grant to Your servants that with all boldness they may speak Your word, 30 by stretching out Your hand to heal and that signs and wonders may be done through the name of Your holy Servant Jesus. 31 And when they had prayed, the place where they were assembled together was shaken; and they were all filled with the Holy Spirit, and they spoke the word of God with boldness."

More Examples from the Bible of God as the Highest Power

In Exodus 7, God instructed Moses and his brother, Aaron to "Show a miracle...take your rod and cast it before Pharaoh, and let it become a serpent." When Aaron did it, Pharaoh called his wise men, sorcerers, and magicians and they did in like manner and their rods turned into serpents also. Therefore, *it did not seem like the God of Moses and Aaron was any greater than the magicians of Pharaoh.*

On the surface, there are other gods, philosophies, or world views that seem to be on the same level as Jesus Christ today. And belief in Jesus Christ seems not to be significantly different than many other religions or spirituality.

However, when and if people really look deeper with an open mind and heart into the claims of Christ and his power to change lives, they will discover how He is truly greater than "a" higher power. God demonstrated his superiority as "Aaron's rod swallowed up all of their rods and as a result, Pharaoh's heart grew hard, and he did not heed them." It seems to me that God is doing miraculous things in the form of healings and deliverances from addictions today. Yes, they are happening daily, and many people have testified about their miraculous deliverances on Christian television, radio, and internet websites and churches. However, most in our religious, spiritual, and humanistic society are not aware of them. Most have mindsets that do not consider listening to or seeking to discover if Jesus Christ is really more than the higher powers that are part of their familiar social circles or networks.

There are dozens of ministers who travel around the world today, preaching the gospel with signs and wonders following them where thousands are healed. I enjoy watching their programs and seeing people share how they have accepted Jesus Christ into their lives and were healed miraculously. The lame and crippled can now walk; the blind see and all sorts of miracles are performed through the name and power of Jesus Christ today. If people will not prejudge or harden their hearts, they can know the reality of Christ that is very much alive and well and active in the lives of believers today. (If you do not know where to look, I have added some resource information links at the end of this book where you will find access to ministries that are actively moving in the supernatural power of God on Earth today.) You can attend their meetings in person or online and see the mighty hand of God at work and sense His presence.

Elijah Versus the Prophets of Baal

I Kings 18 imparts the story of when the prophet Elijah was sent by God to confront 450 prophets of Baal. Elijah came to all the people of Israel and said, "How long will you falter between two opinions? If the Lord is God, follow Him, but if Baal then follow him." But the people answered him not a word. The prophets of Baal cut themselves and called upon Baal for hours to no avail. Then when it was Elijah's turn, he had the people help him and they "repaired the altar of the Lord that was broken down" and poured water on the sacrifice. Then Elijah said, "Hear me, O Lord, hear me, that this people may know that You are the Lord God, and that You have turned their hearts back to You again." Then the fire of the Lord fell and consumed the burnt sacrifice, and the wood and the stones and the dust, and it licked up the water that was in the trench. Now when all the people saw it, they fell on their faces, and they said "The Lord, He is God! The Lord He is God." Thus, defeating the prophets of Baal and the people of Israel acknowledged that God was God and not Baal.

Today, there seem to be many who are not sure whether or not Jesus Christ is Lord of all or just a lord or god among many world religions or spiritual perspectives of today. Unaware that the fire of God fell about 2,000 years ago on the day of Pentecost as recorded in Acts 2, the same phenomenon was experienced at Azusa Street in Los Angeles in the early 1900s. Now, there are literally millions of Spirit-filled Christians all over the world that have been filled or baptized in the Holy Spirit and fire of God.

Most people today do not have a clue that the Holy Spirit that Jesus promised to send is here for those that believe and receive. If more were exposed to and open to the power of the Holy Spirit today, they would know that Jesus Christ is Lord. However, in society today, you may risk verbal persecution if you proclaim that Jesus Christ is Lord without also being willing to acknowledge that Buddha, the wind, Hindu gods Brahma, Vishnu or Shiva, or other powers are on par with Jesus Christ.

There is No Other God That Can Deliver Like This

In Daniel 3, Shadrach, Meshach, and Abed-Nego refused to bow down to a gold image and were thrown into a fiery furnace since they did not serve the gods or worship the gold image that King Nebuchadnezzar made. They reported, "our God whom we serve is able to deliver us from the burning fiery furnace, and He will deliver us from your hand, O king." They were accompanied in the fire by the Son of God who appeared, and the king saw them together. They were delivered without even the smell of smoke on them. Subsequently, the king called Shadrach, Meshach, and Abed-Nego "servants of *the Most High God*." Immediately afterward, the king proclaimed that "there is no other God that can deliver like this." The king even issued a decree that if anyone "speaks anything amiss against the God of Shadrach, Meshach, and Abed-Nego, they shall be cut in pieces, and their houses shall be made an ash heap."

No one can deliver better than Jesus Christ, the son of the living God that has the power to do miraculous things for those who believe and put their trust in him. *Thousands of former alcoholics and drug addicts can and do boldly proclaim that Jesus Christ set them free from their addictions.* Yes, I believe that some people have been and will continue to overcome addiction problems without accepting Jesus Christ as their personal Lord and Savior. However, there truly is no other God that can deliver like this in such a dramatic way that literally changes a person into a new creation, as the Bible says in II Corinthians 5:17.

Resurrection Power

Not only is resurrection taught in the Old Testament, but the theology it teaches us is incredibly profound and speaks to our lives today. The Old Testament of the Bible records accounts of people who arose from the dead thanks to prophets of God:

- I Kings 17:17-24 - The prophet Elijah raised a boy from the dead.

- 2 Kings 4:18-37 - The prophet Elisha raised a boy from the dead.

- 2 Kings 13:20-21 - A dead man came back to life after being thrown on Elisha's dead bones.

- The New Testament of the Bible also has numerous accounts of resurrection.

- Luke 7:11-17 - Jesus encountered a funeral procession and stopped to raise a widow's son from the dead.

- Luke 8:49-56 - Jesus raised a 12-year-old girl from the dead.

- John 11:1-44 - Jesus raised Lazarus from the dead after he was dead for four days.

- According to Mathew 28:1-20; Mark 16:1-20; Luke 24:1-49; and John 20:1 to 21:21-25 - Jesus rose from the dead.

- Matthew 27:50-54 - After Jesus' resurrection from the dead, many godly people who had died earlier were raised to life and appeared to many in Jerusalem.

- Acts 9:36-42 - The apostle Peter prayed and raised Tabitha from the dead.

- Acts 20:7-12 - The apostle Paul raised a young man named Eutychus from the dead.

Of course, the healing powers of faith can do more than restore life. They can also cleanse and heal those who choose to believe.

John the Baptist sent messengers to Jesus, as recorded in Matthew 11:1-6. "Now it came to pass, when Jesus finished commanding His twelve disciples, that He departed from there to teach and to preach in their cities. And when John had heard in prison about the works of Christ, he sent two of his disciples and said to Him, 'Are You the Coming One, or do we look for another?' Jesus answered and said to them, "Go and tell John the things which you hear and see: *The* blind see and *the* lame walk; *the* lepers are cleansed and *the* deaf hear; *the* dead are raised up and *the* poor have the gospel preached to them. And blessed is he who is not offended because of Me."

Jesus Christ performed healings and miracles, including raising the dead. To me, He is greater than any higher power. Today some believers are continuing His ministry by healing people and raising the dead in Jesus' name. Some people have faith that God did miraculous things in the past and will perform miraculous things in the future but have difficulty believing that miracles can and do happen now. Acts 3:12 states, "Nor is there salvation in any other, for there is no other name under heaven given among men by which we must be saved."

- Jesus told His disciples to raise the dead. Consider the following verses and the examples they cite:

- Matthew 10:18 "Heal the sick, cleanse the lepers, raise the dead, cast of demons, freely you received, freely give."

- Matthew 28:18-20 Jesus told His disciples to teach others to do everything He had commanded them, even to the end of the age.

- John 14:12 "Most assuredly, I say to you, he who believes in Me, the works that I do he will do also; and greater works that these he will do, because I go to My Father."

Believers can do greater works than Jesus Christ did while He was bodily present on Earth. Mind-blowing as it may seem to those who do not believe, it is happening today, but many cannot fathom it.

Open your heart and mind for spiritual revelation to operate in the supernatural power of God. Online, you can listen to video testimonies of people that have been raised from the dead.[16] Evangelist Reinhard Bonnke preached to millions in Africa with

---

[16] www.godisreal.today/raised-from-the-dead/

signs and wonders of healings and miracles, including resurrection from the dead.[17] I have personally met three people that have been used by God through the name of Jesus Christ to raise people from the dead. Believe it or not, I know that it is true.

I know many people that have been healed and delivered from addictions. I have personally prayed for people that have been miraculously healed. Most people are not aware of the power of God active and available today. I know of no other higher power that can raise people from the dead or set people free from addictions.

The phenomenon of 'natural recovery'

The mysterious phenomenon of natural recovery also referred to as spontaneous remission and maturing out of addiction, has been studied at least 40 times since 1962. I became aware of this term when I took an Addictive Behaviors course at Casper College in Wyoming in autumn 2003. The professor wrote on a board in front of the class on several occasions about the following recovery rates:

- 65 percent mature out/make a logical decision to stop without getting treatment

- 30 percent quit with help of self-help programs such as AA or NA

- 5 percent get treatment often (seven times for drugs, three times for alcohol)

- Out of that 5 percent:

  - 1 percent stick to their new way of life

  - 1 percent die

This got my attention. Maturing out (another term for natural recovery or spontaneous remission) appears to be the major path to recovery. Natural recovery is a clinical term for the phenomenon of

---

[17] youtube.com/watch?v=MZP5Gq7-WYM

overcoming addiction without professional help. Therefore, I use the term to address this section on recovery rates. However, I believe that most of those that experience natural recovery do so because of the supernatural power of God.

In 2006, I took an Introduction to Research graduate course at the University of Wyoming and decided to do my research project on natural recovery from alcohol and drugs. I discovered that there were about 40 research studies already done on natural recovery. Although the result of the research studies varies as far as the percentage of addicts that experience natural recovery and the possible reasons for it, the fact that many people recover without treatment is undeniable. Why do some people mature out or spontaneously recover and others don't? The precise nature of changes characterizing natural recovery is unclear.

This somewhat mysterious phenomenon of natural recovery was discovered by Charles Winick, a researcher in New York City. He studied public health records of known heroin addicts and noted that those who first became addicts in their late teens ceased to appear on these lists between their mid-twenties and mid-thirties. Only a few died; the others, he discovered, eventually assumed the adult roles they had avoided while they were immersed in their drug habits and environments. Natural recovery of addiction, as observed by Winick, is more typical than not. [18]

Dr. Stanton Peele, a psychologist, recognizes natural recovery from addiction and reports the following: The idea of addiction as inevitably a lifetime burden is a myth. In fact, most people resolve addictions over time and most do so without professional or support-group help.[19] We know this because the American government's own data tells us so. A massive study was carried out by the National Institute on Alcohol Abuse and Alcoholism (NIAAA) in which 43,000 Americans were interviewed about their lifetime substance use. The National Epidemiologic Survey on Alcohol and Related

---

[18] Charles Winick, 1962, Maturing Out of Narcotic Addiction, *Bulletin on Narcotics*, January/March, 1-7.

[19] peele.net

Conditions (NESARC) found that people overwhelmingly overcome drug and alcohol dependencies (their terms for addiction and alcoholism) over the course of their lives:

- 84 percent in the case of nicotine (smoking)

- 91 percent for alcohol

- 97 percent for cannabis (marijuana)

- 99 percent for cocaine

In a *separate analysis,* conducted by NESARC, of subjects who had ever abused or been dependent on a <u>prescription</u> drug (including sedatives, tranquilizers, stimulants, and opioids) over their lifetime, 96 percent stopped using all substances combined. Half the cases remitted between four and five years from the onset of the drug problem. What does all of this mean? In short: people simply rarely spend their entire lives addicted. Given that natural recovery is the norm, how is it possible that we hardly ever hear about it? One reason is that recovery is so commonplace that we don't think anything about it! [20]

To illustrate the vast number of people who are able to overcome addictions on their own (or at least without entering a treatment program or AA), look at research produced by epidemiological investigators for the NIAAA. The National Longitudinal Alcohol Epidemiologic Survey (NLAES) was conducted in 1992 by the US Census Bureau on behalf of the NIAAA.[21] NESARC is the largest survey study of Alcohol Use Disorders ever conducted in the US. Its researchers found that three-fourths of all people with alcohol dependence overcame it and that, of those who did, three fourths or 75 percent did it on their own, without AA or any rehab or treatment program (NIAAA 2009).[22]

---

[20] https://lifeprocessprogram.com/10-guiding-principles-for-maturity-and-natural-recovery/

[21] http://www.niaaa.nih.gov

[22] https://www.niaaa.nih.gov/research/nesarc-iii

Only one-quarter of them did not get better.

New York Times Bestselling author Maia Szalvitz is one of the premier American journalists covering addiction and drugs. She wrote in an article that the idea that addiction is typically a chronic, progressive disease that requires treatment is false, based on evidence. Yet the "aging out" (natural recovery) experience of the majority is ignored by treatment providers and journalists. She reported that most people with addiction simply grow out of it.[23] So, why is this widely denied?

There are many paths to recovery and, if we want to help people get there, we need to explore all of them. That means recognizing that natural recovery exists and not dismissing what we don't like or are unfamiliar with. The good news is that is most people will overcome addictions on their own without a formal rehab program, regardless of what they are addicted to.

Many consider that the "disease" model allows people to feel their addiction is not their fault and that they should seek help to overcome it. In the maturing out or natural approach, people come to see that recovery is a natural process that is more likely than not to occur, as long as they make real progress in the key areas of their lives. The addiction is not lifelong and all-powerful; rather, it is something that ordinary people can surmount.

Natural recovery generally refers to people who overcome diseases even though they either did not receive treatment or did not respond to it. This process is often a mysterious one, like when people recover from cancer or other serious illnesses without explanation. But maturing out of addiction (natural recovery), as observed by Winick, is more typical than not.

"Problematic alcohol use—that is, heavy drinking, or drinking that is accompanied by unpleasant consequences—tends to increase as people go through late adolescence, peaking at about age 22 or

---

[23] https://www.drugfoundation.org.nz/matters-of-substance/matters-of-substance-november-2014/ageing-out-of-addiction/

so, and then decline as they grow older," according to a research paper entitled *Maturing Out of Problematic Alcohol Use* by Patrick M. O'Malley, Ph.D. "Some researchers consider this decline, which has been studied for more than 70 years in many different countries and cultures (Fillmore 1988; Johnstone et al. 1996), a "'maturing out' of problem drinking. This process is believed to result when people reach their twenties and take on the roles and responsibilities of adulthood (Bachman et al. 2002; Yamaguchi and Kandel 1985)."[24]

Supernatural Recovery

My research project at the University of Wyoming was based on the hypothesis that most addicts that experienced natural recovery actually experienced *supernatural recovery* through Jesus Christ. While doing my research, I attended a men's breakfast at Word Christian Fellowship in Casper, Wyoming, where my brother Dan has been pastoring for more than 35 years. I asked the 21 other men present, "How many of you had a serious alcohol or drug problem at one time?" All 21 of them raised a hand, which surprised me. Then I asked if any of them were treated or went to rehab. None of them raised their hands. I asked, "How did you quit?" And all of them said that they gave their life to Jesus. I did not do a DSM diagnosis or some addiction severity index interview to clinically determine or diagnose the degree of their alcohol or drug problems. I believe that there are men and women across the world that have experienced conversion through Christ and attend church regularly who have supernaturally recovered from addictions. A former probation officer told me recently that during all his years as a probation officer, the only probationers on his caseload that quit alcohol and drugs attributed their recovery to giving their lives to Jesus Christ.

Now I realize that many people experience natural recovery in different ways. I have read a couple of stories of celebrities that reported that they quit alcohol and/or drugs when their first child

---

[24] https://pubs.niaaa.nih.gov/publications/arh284/202-204.pdf

was born. Some numerous other motivations and methods have helped addicts recover. As an addiction therapist for almost eight years with the Department of Veterans Affairs, I heard from many veterans that they successfully quit tobacco after years of nicotine addiction by simply deciding one day to quit. Most likely people involved in different religious groups have also experienced natural and/or supernatural recovery.

However, personally, I believe that Jesus Christ has, does, and will continue to supernaturally set addicts totally free. In John 8:36 it says, "So if the Son sets you free you will be free indeed." I also believe that it takes a sincere commitment, submitting to being discipled, and making lifestyle changes to remain free. According to John 14:12, Jesus said "Most assuredly, I say to you, he who believes in Me, the works that I do he will do also; and greater works than these he will do." Jesus Christ healed people from many diseases and afflictions while he was physically present on Earth and now greater works are done in His name through believers today.

Impact of spirituality on treatment outcomes

If you need more proof of the power of faith, consider these separate studies:

- A systematic review of 29 studies from PubMed, CINAHL and Psych Info assessed the role that spirituality and religion play in substance abuse treatment outcomes. *Drug Abuse Treatment Outcome Studies,* funded by the National Institute on Drug Abuse, found religious and spiritual support as motivating factors in successful recovery (Simpson 2003). For most studies, evidence suggested some support for a beneficial relationship between spirituality or religion and recovery from substance use disorders. (Walton-Moss, Ray and Woodruff (John Hopkins) JAN. 2013)

- *Religiousness and spirituality as recovery variables in treated and natural recoveries: A qualitative study.* This study reviews the voluminous empirical evidence on faith's contribution to preventing people from falling victim to substance abuse and helping them recover from it. The study concludes that the value of faith-oriented approaches to substance abuse prevention and recovery is indisputable. (Alcoholism Treatment Quarterly 24 (4): 119-135, 2006. Collins MA.)

- *Belief, Behavior, and Belonging: How Faith is Indispensable in Preventing and Recovering from Substance Abuse*, by <u>Brian J. Grim</u> and <u>Melissa E. Grim</u>, reviewed the ""voluminous empirical evidence on faith's contribution to preventing people from falling victim to substance abuse and helping them recover from it." They found that 73 percent of addiction treatment programs in the U.S.A. include a spirituality-based element, "as embodied in the 12-step programs and fellowships initially popularized by Alcoholics Anonymous, the vast majority of which emphasize reliance on God or a Higher Power to stay sober."[25]

Additionally, *So Help Me God: substance abuse, religion, and spirituality*, a two-year study by Columbia University's National Center on Addiction and Substance Abuse (CASA) examined the link between God, religion, and spirituality, and substance abuse prevention, treatment, and recovery. CASA reviewed more than 300 publications that had examined the link between spirituality, religion, substance abuse, and addiction. The study found that God, religion, and spirituality were key factors for many in the prevention and treatment of their substance abuse and in continuing recovery. (New York, November 2001) I have been an addiction counselor for 30 years and a fully licensed addictions therapist for about the past 20 years. Probably about 90 percent of all addiction treatment models and programs indicate the importance of spirituality in treatment. A higher power "as a person understands it" is usually advocated. To me, Jesus Christ is *greater than a higher power*. Yes,

---

[25] Grim, B.J., Grim, M.E. Belief, Behavior, and Belonging: How Faith is Indispensable in Preventing and Recovering from Substance Abuse. Journal of Religion and Health 58, 1713–1750 (2019).

Jesus Christ, the son of God is a higher power. However, He is much more. I have on several occasions heard people in Alcoholics Anonymous refer to a chair, a light bulb, or a doorknob as their higher power. One man told me that the radiator in his car was his higher power. I have difficulty understanding how an inanimate thing could be considered a higher power. It reminded me of pagan nations mentioned in the Old Testament of the Bible that worshiped idols made of stone or carved wood that could not hear or speak.

If someone mentions that the 12 steps or recovery group that they attend, some philosophy, or religion such as Buddhism or Islam is their higher power, then I can accept that. It seems to me that a higher power should be something bigger, wiser, or more powerful than the person that believes in it. The Bible declares that Jesus Christ is the King of kings and Lord of lords and that one day every knee shall bow and declare it. John 4:4 says, "He who is in you is greater than he who is in the world." Exodus 18:11 cites, "Now I know that the Lord is greater than all the gods." In Psalm 135:5, it states, "For I know that the Lord is great, and our Lord is above all gods."

CHAPTER SIX
THE POWER OF PRISON MINISTRY

While working at Greater Cleveland Teen Challenge, I went on vacation for a week in my hometown. One night, I had a dream that I was preaching in a prison alongside one of my brothers. Imagine my surprise the next day during a revival meeting at Hope Temple when the guest evangelist walked up to me and said, "Young man, God gave you a dream last night and He wants you to obey it." That got my attention. I began thinking, "Why would God call me to prison ministry when surely there is someone more qualified?" I probably looked five or 10 years younger than I was, stood only five-foot-seven, had no tattoos or deep scars on my face. I had never served time in an adult prison. Yes, I was incarcerated in juvenile correctional facilities and the city and county jail, but I had not done any adult prison time. I thought of a list of some really tough and muscular Christian guys who would be better up for the job!

God reminded me of what the Prophet Samuel was told when he went to Jesse's home to pick out one of his sons to become the next king of Israel. In I Samuel 16:7, the Lord said to Samuel, "Do not look at his appearance or the height of his stature…For the Lord does not see as man sees; for man looks at the outward appearance, but the Lord looks at the heart." Then Samuel chose David and anointed him. In verse 12 of the same chapter, the Lord said, "Arise, anoint him, for this is the one." I realized from the dream and the confirmation during the revival service that God truly had called me for prison ministry. I went back to Teen Challenge where I was the program director and told the Rev. Ross. He agreed to replace me as a program director and allow me to become the outreach director so I could do prison ministry and other outreaches.

Prison Ministry

Soon Neil McFarland, a volunteer who used to cut our hair and raise money, took my place at the Perry, Ohio campus. I ministered in prisons and jails across the state of Ohio and won many to Christ over a seven-year period. Several of my brothers came with me to minister at the Ohio State Reformatory in Mansfield, Ohio. One of the many jails that I preached was the Cuyahoga County Jail before they build a new justice center. One day when I walked into the jail, a correctional officer or deputy sheriff told me that the warden wanted to talk to me. As I met him for the first time, he told me that since I have been ministering in the jail, a revival had been going on. All the Bibles were signed out from the library and prayer meetings and Bible studies with singing were going on regularly in the cell blocks. I was surprised. The warden informed me that he appreciated what I had been sharing in jail. I do not take credit for the revival because there were other people ministering in the jails also. However, I give glory and honor to God for choosing me to a part of a life-changing opportunity. Probably more than 80 percent of inmates in jails and prisons have addiction problems that contributed to their criminal behavior. However, Jesus sent me to share the gospel (good news) that totally transformed hundreds of lives. Remember, there is no other God that can deliver in this sort of setting. I could tell many true, inspiring stories regarding prison ministry that I experienced, including this one.

Willie Parish, Jr. entered the Greater Cleveland Teen Challenge program as a heroin addict from Youngstown, Ohio. He was sentenced to prison at the Ohio State Reformatory in Mansfield for a crime he committed prior to entering the program. Since I knew that Willie was genuinely serving the Lord, I asked the chaplains to assign him as a chaplain assistant. One of Willie's duties was to take the new inmates around the prison during orientation. He shared his testimony while walking them around and led many of them to Christ. It reminds me of Joseph in Genesis 39: 21-23: "But the Lord was with Joseph and showed him mercy, and He gave him favor in the sight of the keeper of the prison. And the keeper of the prison committed to Joseph's hand all the prisoners who were in the prison, whatever they did there, it was his doing. The keeper of the prison did not look into anything that was under Joseph's hand, because the Lord was with him; and whatever he did, the Lord made it prosper."

After his release from prison, Willie planted and pastored two churches. At one point, he was the executive director of the Seattle Metro Teen Challenge, and I visited with him there and preached a chapel service to his students. Willie preached at my church in Marietta, Georgia once. We have kept in touch throughout the years. Currently, he is the president of Bread of Life Mission in Seattle. I remember when I first met Willie at Teen Challenge. He asked me, "Is this stuff about Jesus Christ real?" You can see from this brief testimony that Willie believes strongly in Christ and has dedicated his life to serving the Lord and helping others. Years ago, I counted 35 people that I ministered to in prison or that graduated from the Teen Challenge program, that became ministers of the gospel.

There are numerous accounts of people in prison or jail told in the Bible. I especially like Acts 16:25 that describes the Apostle Paul and Silas praying and singing hymns to God at midnight. The prisoners were listening to them and the keeper of the prison, and his family subsequently became believers in Christ. There are also prisons in people's minds – bondage to addictions and mental health disorders – that keep some locked up in negative emotional states. Psalm 142: 1-7 talks about being overwhelmed and depressed with no one caring. A prayer in verse 7 commands, "Bring my soul out of prison, That I may praise Your name." Many people struggling with addictions are overwhelmed and trapped in depression, but the Lord is more than willing and able to bring their souls out of that internal prison and set them free if they call upon Him. Are you or do you know a prisoner that is really listening or reading this book that needs hope and direction to find victory over an addiction or another prison that could benefit? Other references related to prisons include Isaiah 42:7 & 61:1, Psalm 102:20 and 146:7, Hebrews 13:3, and Matthew 25:36.

Open to New Revelation

One day while preaching in the basement of a print shop in a prison where inmates could walk in off of the yard, I had a new revelation experience. That particular day, I was reading the text that I was about to preach from in Luke 4:18-19 that says, "To preach deliverance to the captives and recovery of sight to the blind." While I was reading, I heard the Lord in my spirit say, "Tell them that I will physically heal them today." The thought was outside of my mindset. I thought, "I cannot say that, because if no one gets healed I will look like an idiot." I battled with those thoughts for a couple of minutes, then announced that today God would physically heal anyone that needed healing. I was definitely not in my comfort zone. But I obeyed God.

First, I prayed for a big inmate who had been to the prison hospital a few times due to a chronic stomachache that was still hurting. When I laid hands on him and prayed, he started jumping up and down saying, "I am healed. I am healed. The pain is gone." Then he fell to the floor with a peaceful look. He yelled so loud that he drew in other inmates who were lifting weights out in the yard. Dozens of prisoners got healed and about 50 of them were laying down on the floor worshiping God. I was amazed, along with the inmates. Up to this point, I had preached the gospel of salvation for several years, but I learned that day that salvation also includes healing and deliverance. I opened my mind beyond my preconceived concept and believed God by receiving further revelation anointing for ministry. Now I often pray for people to be healed. I have learned not to put God in a box, or we limit Him and ourselves. It is an exciting adventure in faith to serve God.

Sometimes I did not see immediate effects when I shared Christ in prison. Once I visited with a friend in an honor dorm outside of the walls of a prison. He asked me if I thought that smoking marijuana was wrong for Christians. I told him that I quit smoking marijuana and am now serving the Lord. "What if when you get released, I were to smoke a joint with you?" I offered. He replied, "Then I would think that you are a hypocrite." I smiled. "That answers your question," I told him. A year or two later, when he was released, he drove about 100 miles from Findlay, Ohio to see me in Cleveland, where I was the assistant pastor of a Foursquare church. I was surprised to see him. He told me that he was thinking about his life and the things that I had shared with him about Christ. Then he asked me to pray with him to receive Jesus Christ into his life. Apparently, the seed of the gospel that I had previously shared with him impacted his life. Sometimes we never know the full extent of our influence when we share Christ with others. What if I had not yielded my life to prison ministry for a season? What difference could you make if you share your testimony with others caught up in addiction?

CHAPTER SEVEN

SPIRITUAL KEYS FOR OVERCOMING ADDICTION

The journey toward a new life begins by receiving Jesus Christ into your heart. Understanding the basics of salvation is very important. Romans 10:13 says, "For whoever calls on the name of the Lord shall be saved." The Greek word for saved is *sozo,* and it means salvation in a spiritual sense; rescuing one from a great peril, to protect, keep alive, preserve life, deliver, heal, and be made whole. It includes physical deliverance from the danger of perishing, physical healing from sickness, and deliverance from demonic possession. Therefore, it signifies much more than salvation to escape Hell and go to Heaven. It includes deliverance from addiction also.

Victory over addictions through Christ usually begins with hearing the gospel, which means good news. Romans 10:17 says, "So then faith *comes* by hearing, and hearing by the word of God." It starts by hearing the word of God, then believing and confessing with your mouth. Romans 10:9-10 says "that if you confess with your mouth the Lord Jesus and believe in your heart that God has raised Him from the dead, you will be saved. For with the heart one believes unto righteousness, and with the mouth, confession is made unto salvation."

I have found several ways to tap into spirituality to overcome addictions. Try them in whatever order feels most comfortable for you:

GRACE

Are you ready to be transformed by God's amazing grace? We are saved by believing in this unmerited favor, which we receive thanks to Christ dying on the cross in our place for our sins and iniquities. Ephesians 2:8 says, "For by grace you have been saved through faith, and that not of yourselves; it is the gift of God." In his book *Destined to Reign*, Pastor Joseph Prince said, "Knowing that you are forgiven of all your sins will give you that power to reign over every destructive habit and live a life of victory." God's grace is greater than your addictions. Because of grace, Romans 8:1 says, "There is therefore now no condemnation to those who are in Christ Jesus."

You do not need to live under guilt and condemnation. So many people experienced guilt, shame, and condemnation and then drank alcohol or abused drugs to numb those negative feelings. Others became addicted to substances that influenced them to lie, cheat, steal, and do things they otherwise would not have done. As a result, they became consumed with condemnation. However, now, because of trusting Jesus, Romans 3:22 informs us that we are "the righteousness of God, through faith in Jesus Christ." You can be free from all condemnation. Believe and confess it and you will experience real peace. The word of God will renew your mind and lead you into truths that will set you free.

According to Bible teacher, Andrew Wommack, grace is the power of the gospel. It is not based on what we do but upon what Jesus has already done. When you understand and embrace this message, you will relate to God differently and be forever changed. Grace brings hope and lets us know that we are greatly loved. Having a correct understanding of God and His grace will revolutionize your life.

Due to misinformation and misrepresentation by some pastors, churches, and Christians, a wrong message has been propagated that mistakenly portrays God as angry and ready to send us to Hell. Why would anyone want to serve a God like that? God is full of love and mercy. As an addiction therapist, I am familiar with the theory that addiction is a sin or a character or moral problem in a way that alienates people from wanting anything to do with God. Unfortunately, it is true that God and Christianity have been misrepresented and shared in negative ways. The real truth and knowledge about God are wonderful and pleasantly uplifting and full of grace. All forms of addiction can be overcome with proper knowledge of grace. Jude 22-23 reports that some people are saved with fear while, for some, compassion makes the difference. I serve my savior Jesus Christ because of His love and compassion. Choosing to receive Jesus Christ as your Lord and Savior is the most important decision you'll ever make!

According to Romans 10:9-10, 13, "If thou shalt confess with thy mouth the Lord Jesus, and shalt believe in thine heart that God hath raised him from the dead, thou shalt be saved. For with the heart man believeth unto righteousness; and with the mouth confession is made unto salvation...For whosoever shall call upon the name of the Lord shall be saved." If you would like to receive God's grace, provided by all that Jesus Christ has done for you, and invite Him to be your Savior and Lord, please pray this simple prayer:

"Father God, I thank you for sending your Son, Jesus Christ to die on the cross for my sins. I believe in my heart that Jesus died on the cross, was buried, and rose again from the dead to save me. I repent of my sins and asked for forgiveness and mercy. By faith, I receive Jesus Christ into my heart as my personal savior and lord. Help me to live a victorious and abundant life as a child of God. Thank you for Your love and salvation. Amen."

Read the Bible and Meditate Daily

The Bible is the most popular and the most scrutinized book ever written. It is a guidebook for living victoriously. Psalm 119:105 says "Your word is a lamp to walk by, and a light to illumine my path." 2 Timothy 3:16 says "All scripture is given by inspiration of God, and is profitable for doctrine, for reproof, for correction, for instruction in righteousness." Reading the Bible helps us to know God better.

There is a vast difference between *knowing about* God and personally *knowing* God. Most everyone knows about God, but only a fraction of these personally know Him in an intimate way. The Bible is the foundational truth that teaches us about the true nature of God and His purpose for each of us. Apart from God's Word, mankind would have never learned the all-important message of salvation through our Lord Jesus Christ. Romans 10:17 says, "So faith comes from hearing, and hearing through the word of Christ." 1 Peter 2:2-3 adds, "Like newborn babies, thirst for the pure milk of the word so that by it you may grow in your salvation. Surely you have tasted that the Lord is good!" By reading the Bible on a consistent basis, you can find direction for your life and learn how to best serve the Lord who gave His life for you.

I encourage you to read and study the whole Bible regularly. You can go from desire to delight in reading the Bible. Joshua 1:8-9 says, "Keep this Book of the Law always on your lips; meditate on it day and night, so that you may be careful to do everything written in it. Then you will be prosperous and successful. Have I not commanded you? Be strong and courageous. Do not be afraid; do not be discouraged, for the Lord your God will be with you wherever you go." The Word of God leads us to freedom. Jesus said in John 8:32, "You will know the truth, and the truth will set you free." The truth of God's Word works freedom in many ways and brings joy in all of them. Jesus also said in John 6:63 "The words that I speak to you are Spirit and life." We understand Jesus best when we hear what He has to say and about the life that He has for us.

Knowing God's Word is vital for dealing with temptation

At times, you will be tempted to go back to the bad habits that you have had for years. Focus on staying the course by turning to the pages of the Bible and your relationship with God. Matthew 4:1-

11 relates how Jesus dealt with temptations by the devil. The devil said three times "If you are the Son of God" and Jesus responded to all three temptations by declaring first "It is written" with each particular temptation. The New Testament was not written yet, so Jesus quoted from the Old Testament. From Jesus' example, we learn the importance of knowing the Word of God and how to apply it correctly during temptation. In 1 Corinthians 10:13, it says, "No temptation has overtaken you except such as is common to man, but God is faithful, who will not allow you to be tempted beyond what you are able, but with the temptation will also make the way of escape, that you may be able to bear it."

There are many other scriptural passages that teach us about dealing with temptation. We can overcome all temptations regarding life, including addictive behavior. According to Ephesians 6:17, we need to use "the sword of the Spirit, which is the word of God." We cannot use it unless we study and know the word. I have never used alcohol or drugs in the past 50 years because I have learned to utilize the word of God. Ephesians 6:12 says, "For we do not wrestle against flesh and blood, but against principalities, against power, against the ruler of the darkness of this age, against spiritual hosts of wickedness in the heavenly places." God's word is a powerful tool for defeating all the evil forces against us.

The benefit of Meditation

In Joshua 1:8 The Bible promises success and prosperity to those who meditate on God's Word. **Biblical meditation** is allowing God's Word to control our thoughts. This is important because according to Proverbs 23:7, "As a man thinketh in his heart, so is he." The way we think is one of the most powerful influences on the way we live. Meditation changes your thought life and that will begin to change the rest of your life for the better. Meditation is a very powerful activity. Many religions and non-religious groups use it for living a healthier and less stressful life. **Biblical meditation** is about God and His Word and will help you develop a deeper relationship with God. It will revolutionize your life because you focus on God. The way I meditate on God and His Word is to think of a Scripture passage over and over to let it sink in as I ponder different ways I can apply that Scripture to my life. You will be amazed at the insights for living that you will gain from this method. Meditation benefits both our physical and emotional health and gives us a sense of well-being and peace.

You can try these passages initially before finding others that speak to you:

- Psalm 19:14: "May these words of my mouth and this meditation of my heart be pleasing in your sight, LORD, my Rock and my Redeemer."

- Psalm 104:34: "May my meditation be pleasing to him, as I rejoice in the LORD."

- Psalm 1:1-6 1: "Blessed is the one who does not walk in step with the wicked or stand in the way that sinners take or sit in the company of mockers, but whose delight is in the law of the LORD, and who meditates on his law day and night. That person is like a tree planted by streams of water, which yields its fruit in season and whose leaf does not wither – whatever they do prospers. Not so the wicked! They are like chaff that the wind blows away. Therefore, the wicked will not stand in the judgment, nor sinners in the assembly of the righteous. For the LORD watches over the way of the righteous, but the way of the wicked leads to destruction."

The power of confession

Why does a positive confession matter? Words have power. Proverbs 18:21 says, "Death and life are in the power of the tongue." Our words have supernatural powers that change circumstances and shape destinies. Words can hurt or they can bless. In Numbers 13, Moses sent 12 leaders to investigate or spy out the promised land of Canaan. The men returned with grapes and other fruits and reported that the land flowed with milk and honey. However, they reported that there were giants of great stature in the land. Two of the spies, Joshua and Caleb, said, "Let us go at once and take possession, for we are well able to overcome it." However, the other 10 spies reported, "We are not able to go up against the people, for they are stronger than we." The 10 gave a bad report and said in verse 33, "There we saw the giants; and we were like a grasshopper in our own sight, and so we were in their sight." Notice their confession "we are not able....and we were like a grasshopper in our own sight." Their confession was that they were like grasshoppers (bugs) in their own sight. The very next chapter tells how their negative confession basically discouraged the people from possessing the promised land at the time. Personally, I have developed an attitude that God is with me, and everywhere the souls of my feet step, I bring God's presence and light with me. I no longer have a grasshopper mentality.

What we believe and confess is very important in the way we view and live life. In Joel 3:10, it says, "Let the weak say, I am strong." Words are spiritual; they carry power. Romans 4:17 says that God "calls those things which do not exist as though they did." If your confession for years is that you are an alcoholic or drug addict, and you believe that in your heart, you will probably continue to live with that belief. I think it is beneficial for addicted people to break through denial and realize that they have an addiction. However, once someone admits the addiction, they can grow to a place where they do not think of themselves as addicts or confess it anymore.

Jesus told Simon in John 1:42, "You are Simon, the son of Jonah. You shall be called Cephas" (which is translated as a stone, or Peter). Notice Jesus told him you are Simon, meaning (a reed blowing in the wind), but you shall be Peter (a stone). Confession of the Word of God isn't lying when we are agreeing with what God says, even if it has not come to pass yet. Proverbs 12:14 tells us that we shall be satisfied with good by the fruit of our mouths. In Genesis 19:5-16, God gave Abram and Sarai new names. Abram's name was changed to Abraham, meaning the father of many nations, and Saria's name was changed to Sarah, meaning the mother of many nations. They were old and childless, yet God had plans for their lives. Can you imagine going around and introducing yourself as Abraham, the father of many nations, or as Sarah, mother of many nations while being old, without a child, and past childbearing age? However, they confessed their names for years before they had a child because they believed in God. Most people know the rest of the story. They called themselves what God told them to and they eventually had a child. That is like the weak saying "I am strong" when in the natural it seems untrue. The secular world acknowledges that if people hear negative things spoken about them – such as you are stupid or worthless – that it can become a self-fulfilling prophesy if you believe it. I maintain that we can say positive things about ourselves that we can internalize and reap the benefits of our confessions. I do not confess that I am an alcoholic or a drug addict. I believe that I am completely cured. I am not *in recovery*, I am *recovered*. See the power in that small difference in wording?

One of my brothers told me that soon after turning his life over to the Lord, he quit alcohol and drugs but struggled to give up smoking cigarettes. He told me that he began looking in a mirror daily and confessing, "I am free from smoking cigarettes. I am tobacco-free." And he was able to quit. He knew a guy who was addicted to cocaine and instructed him to look into a mirror regularly and confess "I no longer use cocaine. I am free from cocaine." In a few weeks, he quit using cocaine. There is power in confession. Remember, we can call those things that be not as though they are. You are not telling a lie. You are speaking to your future.

When we confess what God says about us, we are telling the truth before the results are manifest. In Judges 6, an angel of the Lord found Gideon hiding and told him "The Lord is with you, you mighty man of valor." Gideon responded with doubt by stating he was the least of the members of his family. However, he became a mighty man of valor and lead a group to victory against great odds to deliver people from enemies that had stolen from them for years.

Genesis 27, 28, and 32 shares how Jacob deceived his blind father Isaac to gain his blessing that was meant for Esau, Jacob's older brother. Jacob had an encounter with God and God changed his name from Jacob, meaning *deceiver*, to Israel, prince with God. Today, people know about Israel, who was blessed with a new name.

Let's let go of our past mistakes and confess a new and better future free from deception and addictive behavior.

One of the tools that people in addiction recovery use is affirmation. Positive affirmations are short, positive statements that you repeat over and over. The aim is for them to enter the subconscious mind and change the way you think and, in turn, the way you behave. Positive affirmations are often taught in therapy sessions to help clients improve their self-esteem or boost their confidence. Clients are encouraged to use positive self-affirmations to help themselves overcome obstacles to getting better. They can say things such as "I am free from drug addiction; all desire for (alcohol or whatever addiction) has left me and I am free; I am becoming a better person", etc. You can make up your own affirmation to confess. Ideally, it should be something you use numerous times daily for a long period of time so it becomes embedded in your mind and changes your thought patterns. The power of daily affirmations involves cultivating a positive mind and setting your intentions for a victorious life. Words are powerful and affirmations can help you get to where you want to go in recovery from addiction.

Years ago, I heard that when a baby elephant was born in a circus family, a chain was secured around one of its legs. At the other end of the chain, a metal stake was pounded into the ground to keep the little elephant from wandering off. The calf often tugged to get free, however, and the chain caused pain when he pulled on it. The little elephant got the message not to tug because it hurt. Eventually, he quit trying as his mind convinced him that he could not get free. When the animal grew into a massive, powerful elephant with thicker skin, he still had the same chain and stake. He could have easily pulled up the stake and walked around wherever he desired, but he never did because he was conditioned not to pull. Maybe you have tried before to break away from addiction and failed, but you are wiser now and you can break away with the proper mindset and motivation.

Do not believe that you will remain stuck in addiction. Philippians 4:13 says, "I can do all things through Christ who strengthens me." Never again will I confess defeat, for 2 Corinthians 2:14 tells me, "God always causes me to triumph in Christ Jesus." The confession of our mouths will eventually bring forth the things we speak. The process of believing and speaking is what brings every benefit of our salvation promised in God's Word from Heaven into our lives. Words reveal what we truly believe. Jesus said, in Matthew 12:34-37, "Out of the abundance of the heart the mouth speaks...By thy Words thou shalt be justified, and by thy words thou shalt be condemned." That is why it is so important to say what God has said. How do we give glory to God? By honoring the Words He has spoken and demonstrating our trust in Him. Our first step of acting on our faith in His Word is to agree with and say the things He has said.

Forgiveness

Forgiveness is the act of pardoning an offender. In the Bible, the Greek word translated "forgiveness" literally means "to let go." Jesus taught his followers to pray in Luke 11:4: "Forgive us our sins, for we, ourselves also forgive everyone who is in debt to us." We forgive others when we let go of resentment and give up any claim to be compensated for the hurt or loss we have suffered. We are not excusing or condoning the wrong as though it never happened, but we let go of it so it will not affect us negatively in our physical or mental health.

Formula for Forgiveness

I have adopted the following formula for forgiveness, and it works well for me. In Luke 6:27-38, Jesus said:

"But I say to you who hear: Love your enemies, do good to those who hate you, bless those who curse you, and pray for those who spitefully use you. To him who strikes you on the one cheek, offer the other also. And from him who takes away your cloak, do not withhold your tunic either. Give to everyone who asks of you. And from him who takes away your goods do not ask them back. And just as you want men to do to you, you also do to them likewise. But if

you love those who love you, what credit is that to you? For even sinners love those who love them. And if you do good to those who do good to you, what credit is that to you? For even sinners do the same. And if you lend to those from whom you hope to receive back, what credit is that to you? For even sinners lend to sinners to receive as much back. But love your enemies, do good, and lend, hoping for nothing in return; and your reward will be great, and you will be sons of the Most High. For He is kind to the unthankful and evil. Therefore, be merciful, just as your Father also is merciful. Judge not, and you shall not be judged. Condemn not, and you shall not be condemned. Forgive, and you will be forgiven. Give, and it will be given to you: good measure, pressed down, shaken together, and running over will be put into your bosom. For with the same measure that you use, it will be measured back to you."

Jesus tells us how to treat enemies, and, from that, I have learned principles for forgiveness. We are to love, do good, bless, and pray for enemies. Believe me, I have been treated very badly and hurt deeply. However, I use these four principles to let bygones be bygones. It is not in my nature to absolve people that have done me wrong, but I know that I will not be forgiven if I do not forgive others. Therefore, I pray, "Father God, in obedience to you and as an act of my will I choose to forgive [name of the person(s)]. Give me the grace to love them, do good to them, bless them, and pray for them." Then I pray about how I can do something good for them. I bless them whenever I think of them and pray from them. I may feel like blessing them with a brick to their heads, but I choose to forgive and obey the Lord. I pray that the person(s) will experience salvation and go to Heaven. This process protects me from having a root of bitterness as mentioned in Hebrews 12:15: "Looking carefully lest anyone fall short of the grace of God; lest any root of bitterness springing up cause trouble, and by this many become defiled." It takes the sting out of the offense that has been done. I let go of the offense and focus on positive things, knowing that I am heeding. Proverbs 4:23 says, "Keep your heart with all diligence, For out of it *spring* the issues of life." I can go through life without focusing on negative things that could influence me to go back to addictive thinking and behaviors, but I choose this approach instead.

Does forgiveness mean the person who wronged you does not have to take responsibility for their actions? No, but you will be free from the thoughts of hatred and bitterness. Forgiveness is not only done for the sake of the one you are forgiving, but for your own sake so that you do not have to live with ongoing negative feelings. The fact that you forgive someone does not condone what they have done, nor does it by any means make it all right. We are told to love our enemies, but we are not required to trust them or have them as our friends. Forgiveness is a choice to let go of the past and not permit thoughts of hatred to rule your mind. According to Matthew 6:14-16 and other verses, the Bible instructs us to forgive as the Lord forgave us. We forgive <u>by faith</u>, out of obedience.

Since forgiveness goes against our nature, we must forgive by faith, whether we feel like it or not. Since Christ forgave us for our sins and wrongdoings, we should forgive ourselves and others for wrongdoings. Do you need to forgive yourself? Is there anyone that you want forgiveness from? Who do you need to forgive? Are you holding on to any resentment? Holding a grudge or resentment could feed addictive behavior.

Discipleship through Relationships

During Jesus' earthly ministry, and during the days of the early church, the term that was used most frequently to designate one of Jesus' followers was *disciple,* the Greek word that means *to learn.* Historically, the word recognizes a pupil-teacher relationship. By looking at Jesus' ministry, we see how His relationship with His disciples modeled that type of relationship. Jesus poured Himself into those who would multiply through leadership by teaching His disciples, spending intimate relational time with them, and sending them out to proclaim the gospel and do good works. Jesus staked His whole ministry on creating disciples.

As we read further in the New Testament, we see the Apostle Paul carry on the process of training disciples. His relationship with a young Christian named Timothy is evident throughout the epistles. He wrote to Timothy in 2 Timothy 2:2, "And the things you have heard me say in the presence of many witnesses entrust to reliable people who will also be qualified to teach others." Paul poured his life into Timothy by modeling to him the importance of discipleship and encouraging him to continue the process. Discipling takes a commitment of time and energy to personally teach and show believers how to grow in faith and apply God's Word to their lives in practical ways. The mission and purpose of the church are to equip and grow disciples who, in turn, will disciple others.

Unfortunately, many churches today have neglected to make disciples. Therefore, new believers with addiction or other problems are not given thorough guidance on how to live an overcoming life. I believe that people with life-controlling problems like addiction need to be discipled by a mature or seasoned believer. Whereas, some Christians that have not experienced a life-controlling problem may be able to attend church once a week and not backslide. I believe those that have struggled with addiction issues need to attend church services as often as possible and volunteer to serve people in the church on a regular basis.

As we study the Great Commission and examine the practical ministry models of Jesus and the Apostle Paul, we can realize that discipleship consists of pouring into others. We must train them in the Word, in a healthy relationship, and in ministry, so that they might develop as healthy believers who can walk by faith, share their faith, and multiply their faith. Through His Great Commission in Matthew 28:16-20, Jesus focuses his followers on the ongoing importance of discipleship through the ages and declares the responsibility of disciples toward the world to make disciples of all the nations. Discipling others means mentoring them in the faith. Discipleship teaches Biblical precepts while modeling and guiding others toward living victoriously as followers of Jesus Christ.

The main characteristic of being a disciple (a student or pupil) is to develop an intimate relationship with Christ rather than just learning about Him. Jesus Christ and the abundant life He offers are often misunderstood by those that have not been discipled in the faith. How will new believers with addiction issues learn how to handle life's struggles without encouragement, wisdom, and guidance from someone that has learned through experience what to do in different situations? Find someone to disciple you and you can avoid struggles or learn how to deal with them effectively. It has been great to have relationships with people that have mentored me in this way. They have provided great guidance. Without being discipled, I would probably be floundering in my spiritual life and would not have learned to handle important life challenges effectively.

Praise and Worship

The Bible tells us that God inhabits the praise of His people in Psalm 22:3. Personally, I love to sense the Lord's presence—it is better than any feelings that alcohol and drugs ever provided for me. Psalm 150: 6 tells us, "Let everything that has breath praise the Lord." Psalm 9:1-3 adds, "I will praise You, O Lord, with my whole heart; I will tell of all Your marvelous works. I will be glad and rejoice in You; I will sing praise to Your name, O Most High." Psalm 18: 2-3 says "The Lord is my rock and my fortress and my deliverer; My God, my strength, in whom I will trust; My shield and the horn of my salvation, my stronghold. I will call upon the Lord, who is worthy to be praised; So shall I be saved from my enemies."

There is such power in praise. Praise is an outward expression, not just to God but in order to let others know how good God is. True praise comes from deep in the heart. The outcome is that others become aware of God working in us and encourages them to trust God also. Psalm 40 talks about being brought out of a horrible pit of the miry clay (addiction can be described as a horrible pit), being set on a rock, and following steps established by God so that God can put a new song of praise in my mouth. Then many hear the praise and trust in the Lord. It also says, "Let all those who seek You rejoice and be glad in You; Let such as love your salvation say continually, The Lord be magnified." If more people that have experienced God's deliverance from addiction and other problems will boldly praise God, then many others will also trust God and also be saved.

Praise Defeats Enemies

Praise defeated enemies in 2 Chronicles 20:14-22 as the people of God were surrounded by armies that far outnumbered them. They sent a choir out before the army, singing "Praise the Lord, for His mercy endures forever." When they began to sing and to praise, the Lord set ambushes against the enemy armies and they were defeated. We may not understand how praise works, but it does. I challenge you to become a person of genuine praise so you can experience the release of the power of God to deliver you. There are seven different Hebrew words for praise used in the Old testament. I encourage you to research praise and worship that can enlighten you richly and revolutionize your life when you learn to apply them. Most people have not discovered the supernatural power of praise that is available. It is well worth the investment of time.

Worship

Worship in the Bible, in both the original Hebrew and Greek, conveys the idea of "to prostrate oneself, to bow down, to fall face down, to pay homage and to pay respect." It involves humbling ourselves and bowing low before the Lord, not just physically, but in our hearts. Worship is the highest form of honor and respect that we can show towards God. While worship is often done in public, its main purpose is somewhat different from praise. Worship is a direct conversation between you and God. It is highly intimate and personal. Worship is for an audience of one—God. The more time we spend truly worshiping Him, the more intimate our relationship and friendship with Him will be.

In John 4:23-24, Jesus said that "true worshipers will worship the Father in spirit and truth; for the Father is seeking such to worship Him. God is Spirit, and those who worship Him must worship in spirit and truth." It is very precious when we take the time to be genuinely quiet as God speaks to us. The God that created the universe desires to be intimate with each of us. It takes sincerely seeking the Lord and waiting upon Him, but the benefit is wonderful.

87

The Power of Praise and Worship

Praise and worship are important for all Christians, but I believe that believers who have struggled with life-controlling problems such as addictions need to press in and develop a strong praise-and-worship lifestyle. Praise should be an integral part of our lives at home, at work, in our car, or anywhere else. In Psalm 34:1, David said, "I will bless the Lord at all times; His praise shall continually be in my mouth." In Luke 17:11-19 Jesus healed ten lepers, but only one returned to give glory to God by falling on his face to give thanks. I, for one, am grateful for all that God has done for me, my family, and friends. I praise and worship Him regularly. Does God deserve our best praise for all the things He has done? I could share numerous more Bible verses regarding praise and worship and tell marvelous details of things God has done in my life. He can easily do the same for you once you let him into your heart.

Receive the Power the Holy Spirit

The supernatural power of the Holy Spirit is available to empower you. The Holy Spirit can give you the power to be victorious over addiction, loneliness, depression, anxiety, and more. Most Christians don't ascribe nearly enough importance to the Holy Spirit and what He is doing on Earth today. In Genesis 1:1-2, the Bible says, "In the beginning God created the heaven and the earth. And the earth was without form, and void; and darkness was upon the face of the deep. And the Spirit of God moved upon the face of the waters." The Holy Spirit was present at creation. Jesus did not do any miracles until He had been anointed with the Holy Spirit, and Jesus told His disciples that they would receive power after they receive the Holy Spirit. Much of modern-day Christianity views the born-again experience as if that is all there is to salvation.

In Luke 24:49, Jesus said, "Behold, I send the Promise of My Father upon you; but tarry in the city of Jerusalem until you are endued with power from on high." Jesus added in John 14:16, "And I will pray the Father, and He will give you another Helper, that He may abide with you forever." In John 14:26, Jesus identified the helper: "But the Helper, the Holy Spirit, whom the Father will send in My name, He will teach you all things, and bring to your remembrance all things that I said to you." Jesus said in Acts 1:8: "But you shall receive power when the Holy Spirit has come upon you; and you shall be witnesses to Me in Jerusalem, and in all Judea and Samaria, and to the end of the Earth." The Greek word for power in Acts 1:8 is *dunamis*, meaning force, miraculous power, strength, or ability. The dynamite power of the Holy Spirit is available for us forever to help us in all areas of our life.

According to Acts 2:1-47, on the Day of Pentecost 120 disciples in verse 4 "were all filled with the Holy Spirit and began to speak with other tongues, as the Spirit gave them utterance." In verses 5-12, a multitude of people from every nation heard the sound and was amazed and marveled because everyone heard them speak in his own language. They wondered, "Whatever could this mean?" In verses 13-18, the crowd thought the disciples were intoxicated. The Apostle Peter informed them that they were not drunk by wine, but by fulfillment of the Prophet Joel's prophecy. "And it shall come to pass in the last days, says God, That I will pour out of My Spirit on all flesh; Your sons and your daughters shall prophesy, Your young men shall see visions, Your old men shall dream dreams. And on My menservants and on My maidservants, I will pour out My Spirit in those days; And they shall prophesy." In verses 38 & 39, Peter said to them, "Repent, and let every one of you be baptized in the name of Jesus Christ for the remission of sins; and you shall receive the gift of the Holy Spirit. For the promise is to you and to your children, and to all who are afar off, as many as the Lord our God will call."

The disciples in the upper room received the promise that Jesus told them to wait for. They were filled or baptized with the Holy Spirit and became bold witnesses. The baptism in the Holy Spirit is a spiritual experience that God wants all of His children to have. It is also called "being filled with the Spirit." Remember that the Holy Spirit has the same nature as God the Father and the Lord Jesus Christ. Baptism in the Holy Spirit is one of the most vital things for any Christian serious about being all they can be in God and doing all they are supposed to be able to do in God. This baptism is essential for fully knowing God and making Him known.

In Acts 19:1-7, the Apostle Paul met some Christians in Ephesus who were not aware of the Holy Spirit. "And it happened, while Apollos was at Corinth, that Paul, having passed through the upper regions, came to Ephesus. And finding some disciples, he said to them, 'Did you receive the Holy Spirit when you believed?' So, they said to him, 'We have not so much as heard whether there is a Holy Spirit.' And he said to them, 'Into what then were you baptized?' So, they said, 'Into John's baptism.' Then Paul said, 'John indeed baptized with a baptism of repentance, saying to the people that they should believe on Him who would come after him, that is, on Christ Jesus.' When they heard this, they were baptized in the name of the Lord Jesus. And when Paul had laid hands on them, the Holy Spirit came upon them, and they spoke with tongues and prophesied. Now the men were about twelve in all."

There are many other examples in the Bible of people being filled with the Holy Spirit, but I will not take time to list them all. We need to know that the Holy Spirit is available for each of us. A Christian without power is a Christian that needs the baptism of the Holy Spirit.

Receiving the infilling or baptism of the Holy Spirit opened up a whole new, dynamic relationship with the Lord for me. 1 Corinthians 12:7-10 says, "But the manifestation of the Spirit is given to each one for the profit of all: for to one is given the word of wisdom through the Spirit, to another the word of knowledge through the same Spirit, to another faith by the same Spirit, to another gift of healings by the same Spirit, to another the working of miracles, to another prophecy, to another discerning of spirits, to another different kind of tongues, to another the interpretation of tongues."

I have experienced some of these gifts operating in my life, such as prophecy, speaking in other tongues, interpretation of tongues, word of wisdom, and word of knowledge. It is my desire that you experience that same power of the Holy Spirit and the gifts that come with it. You will become more profitable to others utilizing the gifts of the Spirit. Personally, I speak in tongues every day for many reasons, including it helps me intercede according to the will of God (Romans 8:26-27) and edifies or builds me up in the faith (1 Corinthians 14:4 & Jude 20).

Say this prayer if you sincerely desire to receive the baptism in God's Holy Spirit:

"Heavenly Father, I come to You. I thank You that Jesus saved me. I recognize my need for the power of the Holy Spirit to live victoriously. I pray that the Holy Spirit will come upon me and fill me now as promised. I receive the baptism in the Holy Spirit right now by faith in Your Word. Thank You, Lord, for baptizing me in Your Holy Spirit. Amen."

Prayer

Prayer is vital for spiritual growth and it is an altogether wonderful activity. It allows you to talk to God and listen to Him. Prayer is not complicated or difficult. In Luke 11:1-4, one of his disciples asked Jesus to teach his disciples to pray. What is often referred to as the Lord's Prayer was recorded. I like to start my prayer with thanksgiving and praise due to my understanding of Psalm 100:4: "Enter into His gates with thanksgiving, and into His courts with praise."

I used to beg God to do things in prayer. However, I have learned to pray the answer instead of the problem. For instance, when I face financial needs, instead of begging God to help me pay a bill or something, now I remind God that He is Jehovah Jireh that sees and provides. He owns the cattle on 1,000 hills, He will open up the windows of Heaven because I pay tithes and give offerings regularly. He will supply all my needs, according to His riches in glory. Therefore, I pray in faith, and when I finish praying I feel great anticipation and confidence knowing that God is faithful and will meet my need. When I begged, I used to finish praying with a sense of doubt or uncertainty. The Bible instructs us to pray to God the Father in Jesus' name, so I do that. I know that God enjoys fellowship with us.

When I was a student at Teen Challenge, I spent a couple of hours per day on my knees in the prayer room. I sought the Lord with all my heart. Rev. Wilkerson, the founder of Teen Challenge, had a brother in the program while I was there. I remember Jerry Wilkerson telling me when I first met him that his brother David told him to start every day with prayer by waking up an hour before everyone else, and he did. When I joined Rev. Ross to start Greater Cleveland Teen Challenge, Jerry and his wife, Evelyn, worked on the staff with me. Jerry never returned to drinking alcohol and faithfully maintained his prayer life and relationship with the Lord. He became a great leader in the ministry.

During Bible college, I continued my prayer life in a prayer room there. A couple of times the dean, who lived above me, came down and asked me to pray more quietly so he could sleep. The Lord has blessed me tremendously and given me much encouragement, comfort, and guidance through prayer. During the summer of 1970 at Harrisburg Teen Challenge, I had a couple of unique experiences. While sleeping, I literally heard a loud booming voice in my room that said "Pray." It kind of freaked me out, but I got up, turned on my light, got on my knees, and prayed. Maybe a week later I heard that same command as I was waking up out of a sound sleep. Of course, I got up and prayed. I did not know what I was praying about, so I prayed in tongues.

After about 30 minutes, a student knocked on my door. While sleeping downstairs in the living room, he heard footsteps at the front door, and dismissed it. But he eventually got up, opened the door, and found a note. It was from a guy that I had witnessed to that day; he wrote that he decided to go jump off a bridge to kill himself. Then I knew why God woke me up to pray. So, the student and I prayed more and went back to sleep. A couple of days later, the young man who left the note came by the Center to talk to me. Obviously, he did not jump off the bridge. He said that he thought more about what I shared with him about Christ and came to see me to give his heart to the Lord. Of course, I led him in a prayer of salvation.

I sound like I was very spiritually attuned to God to hear His voice. Actually, I have never heard His loud voice in all the years since then. God had to speak out loud to get my attention. God speaks to me in different ways now, but I know when he speaks. Jesus said in John 10:27, "My sheep hear my voice, and I know them, and they follow Me." I have a 17-year-old son named Zion. One night I woke up to quickly use the bathroom and I heard the Lord say "Acel is pregnant." (Acel is my wife). I immediately thought, "No, we were not planning on having a child." Then the Lord said, "Be happy" and I responded, "Yes, sir." The next day, my wife could not stand the smell of my cologne. After church and lunch, I told my wife that I was going out to get a newspaper or fill the car up with gasoline. I went to a drugstore and bought a pregnancy test. Then I told my wife that God told me that she was pregnant. She said no because we were careful in our birth-control method. However, at my insistence she took the test and, sure enough, she was pregnant.

I am telling you that God talks to praying people if they learn to understand and listen for His voice. I enjoy praying and hope that you do too. Prayer helps break the power of addiction when we pray in faith.

Get Loaded Daily

I tell people that I get loaded daily because I believe the Bible says in Psalm 68:19: "Blessed *be* the Lord, *Who* daily loads us *with benefits,* The God of our salvation." Every day, I experience being loaded with benefits from God. I purposely load up daily by reading and meditating on the word of God, praising and worshiping, praying, listening to Christian teaching and music, and often sharing fellowship with other believers. Benefits arise such as health, peace, joy, love, purpose, provision of food and shelter, supportive family and friends, etc.

I would probably be dead or in prison if I did not discover the true joy of serving God. I believe that alcohol and drugs are often counterfeits for the presence of the Holy Spirit. Ephesians 5:18 says, "Do not be drunk with wine, in which is dissipation; but be filled with the Spirit." According to Acts 2, on the Day of Pentecost the disciples were filled with the Holy Spirit and some people mocked them as being full of wine, but Peter told them they were not drunk as some supposed. The best high is from the Holy Spirit and not from alcohol or drugs. I have the Holy Spirit within me that blesses me daily with great benefits. I love to sing and pray in the Spirit daily, which fills me with peace and joy. I serve the Lord God most high. Some people have only experienced holy spirts (the original spelling of the word *spurts*) by briefly serving God, or they have had moments of the Lord's presence. However, learning to walk in an ongoing relationship with Him provides benefits that may seem too good to be true. However, they are definitely real because God's word is true, and the Holy *Spirit* is available now and every day.

We can get loaded daily once we have received Christ into our lives and begin to live an abundant life relying on God's grace. All the spiritual keys shared in this book – including reading and meditating on the Bible, confession, forgiveness, prayer, discipleship, praise and worship, the power of the Holy Spirit, desiring spiritual gifts, giving, and witnessing – will transform you into a strong person with supernatural power to overcome addiction and any negative habits. Victory is yours if you will believe and receive what God has for you by getting loaded daily.

CHAPTER EIGHT

TOOLS FOR HELPING OTHERS

G ifts of the Holy Spirit are profitable and real. As you embrace Jesus and the life He wants you to lead, it is rewarding for you and so many others that you share your love and knowledge with others. Countless times in my life, simply opening up to others about the potential for changes in their lives by accepting God into their hearts has changed the paths that others have followed. 1 Corinthians 14 talks about spiritual gifts, and verse 1 by saying, "Pursue love, and desire spiritual gifts, but especially that you may prophesy." There are many ways that you can share your gifts, as I have shared mine. Let me tell you about some of the life-changing experiences I have had as I passed on what I had learned to other people, who then became disciples as well.

Once I had found my path, I developed a strong desire to help others get free from addictions. I sensed a call to ministry and attended Trinity Bible Institute (now Trinity Bible College and Graduate School) in North Dakota for two quarters in 1970. During the summer of 1970, I was the resident director of Teen Challenge in Harrisburg, Pennsylvania which had 15 students in the program. I worked as program director and outreach director at Greater Cleveland Teen Challenge in Ohio from January 1971 to August 1979, then as assistant director and executive director at Teen Challenge of Louisiana from April 1981 to May 1984. I have been doing monthly volunteer work at Greater Piedmont Teen Challenge in Greensboro, North Carolina from 2013 to the present and am now serving on their advisory board. Therefore, I have been involved in the ministry of Teen Challenge for about 20 years and have seen countless lives changed.

Understand the 'fake' high and find a better approach

Based on my experience, alcohol and drugs are facsimiles for being filled with the Holy Spirit. I remember at times being high on speed (amphetamines), plus marijuana or hashish, while my friends would talk for hours about ways to solve world problems. We thought we had inspired ideas that were full of wisdom. However, the next day we could not remember the solutions that we had come up with the night before.

Methamphetamine addicts often imagine themselves as being very smart when they are high and feeling bold and confident in themselves. This represents a fake sense of knowledge. Addicts addicted to pain pills (opioids) often believe that they are functioning at an amazing level by working faster or accomplishing more and thinking better, when actually they are deceived by the drug high and are less productive. A pain pill addict once shared in a recovery group that I facilitated that he was at home with his wife and children and thought he was acting fine and in control. But his wife videotaped him and showed it to him. He was shocked at what he saw. Often people high on alcohol and drugs think there are functioning well, but others can see that they are not. The Holy Spirit helps us function at a high level in which we are engaged in conversations and behaviors that are peaceful and in control. Alcoholic or drug-addicted parents can be home with their families and be disengaged as far as healthy interactions. When they are present, but disconnected, for years due to addiction, it affects their children for many years and often for the rest of their lives.

Adult children of alcoholics and drug addicts often grow up with a sense of abandonment that affects their self-images. Alcohol – often called spirits – and drugs cannot compare to the benefits of being filled with the Holy Spirit. There are many negative consequences as a result of intoxicating chemicals, such as poor judgment, loss of productivity, social and emotional non-engagement, possible legal and financial problems, health problems, etc. God has provided us a free, inexhaustible source of power to live the Christian life free from addictions. When a person is filled with the Holy Spirit, he or she is transformed to exhibit love and the fruits of the Spirit. Galatians 5:23 says, "the fruit of the Spirit is love, joy, peace, long suffering, kindness, goodness, faithfulness, gentleness, self-control." I think that all caring human beings should desire the fruits of the Spirit instead of being angry, belligerent, mean, miserable, bad, anxious, or out of control.

Galatians 5:16-25 says, "Walk in the Spirit, and you shall not fulfill the lust of the flesh. For the flesh lusts against the Spirit, and the Spirit against the flesh; and these are contrary to one another so that you do not do the things that you wish. But if you are led by the Spirit, you are not under the law. Now the works of the flesh are evident, which are: adultery, fornication, uncleanness, lewdness, idolatry, sorcery, hatred, contentions, jealousies, outbursts of wrath, selfish ambitions, dissensions, heresies, envy, murders, drunkenness, revelries, and the like; of which I tell you beforehand, just as I also told you in time past, that those who practice such things will not inherit the kingdom of God. But the fruit of the Spirit is love, joy, peace, long suffering, kindness, goodness, faithfulness, gentleness, self-control. Against such, there is no law. And those who are Christ's have crucified the flesh with its passions and desires. If we live in the Spirit, let us also walk in the Spirit."

Often addicts end up emulating the works of the flesh that are contrary to walking in the Spirit. Under the influence of mood-altering chemicals that affect behavior, addicts sometimes do things that they would never do when sober-minded, such as arguing, fighting, or having sexual escapades with someone other than their spouse or partner. Do not jeopardize your reputation, family, employment, financial situation, or physical or mental health by continuing in addiction. A veteran once told me that he lost his successful business, his marriage, and his freedom and ended up in jail. He told me that his uncle visited him in jail and told him point-blank that he had lost it all due to drinking too much alcohol. The veteran informed me that a light bulb in his head lit up and, for the first time, he realized that alcohol was destroying his life. Some people romance their alcohol or drug of choice and treat it like a friend while staying in denial. Sometimes, they never admit their problem and eventually experience catastrophic results. Some addicts do not believe they can change or even desire to do so.

There are many reasons why people become addicted. Often, there is an underlying issue that fuels addiction, such as trauma or low self-esteem. However, once a person becomes hooked, then the addiction can take on a life of its own. For instance, taking prescribed pain pills as a result of a serious injury, or drinking alcohol to relieve stress, can turn into an addiction that is hard to shake without the supernatural power of the Holy Spirit. People's reactions to various types of alcohol and drugs are often different. Some people love cocaine, heroin, marijuana, or a certain type of alcohol the first time they try it, while others try a specific substance once and hate it. Some use to calm their anxieties and fears, but the high does not last and soon they need to use more to get the desired effect. Some temporarily are able to relax, cope with stress and frustration, or be less inhibited and more sociable. They forget shame or pain, or they release suppressed emotions after consuming alcohol and drugs. Some aim to numb unpleasant thoughts and feelings, but the Holy Spirit provides a better way when we learn how to walk in the Spirit. The Holy Spirit gives comfort, peace, and joy without negative side effects.

Giving

When people love, they give their time, strength, and finances to what they care about. If you think about it, many people waste their time, energy, and money on addiction-related activities. John 3:16 says, "For God so loved the world that He gave His only begotten Son, that whosoever believes in Him, should not perish but have everlasting life." Volunteering is a great way to give to good causes that help people. Read Malachi 3:8-10 and you will realize that giving is important to God as an avenue to bless us. Check the pages of Luke 6:38 and see what Jesus said about giving. Read 2

Corinthians 9:6-7 to see the Apostle Paul's view on generosity.

When the chains of addiction are broken, we are free to give cheerfully. It is truly more blessed to give than to receive. I love to give, and I hope you do too. It brings joy to us and the ones that we bless. When we give of our time, prayer, energy, and money, it helps to take our minds off of addictive thinking and activities. Giving of ourselves to good causes for which we have a passion enriches our lives and aids in putting addiction in the rear view mirror of our lives. I encourage you to be a giver by coaching a youth sports team, teaching a Sunday School class, volunteering at a senior citizen's home, etc. When the ones that you are serving see you faithfully serving, their faces will light up in appreciation for you, which in turn will give you a great feeling of purpose.

I have often picked up hitchhikers to give them a ride. You never know how a conversation in your car will lead to opening a doorway for them or you. Once, I was headed to visit someone in jail when an addict asked me to give him a ride across Cleveland so he could get his dose of methadone. Then he asked me to pick him up at the methadone clinic when I was done. When I stopped by to get him, I could not find him. Meanwhile, another addict asked me to give him a ride back to the west side. While driving, I saw the tip of an ice pick in his shirt sleeve, so I asked him about it. He told me that he had been shot and stabbed several times and showed me the scars to prove it. I talked to him about Jesus Christ as the highest power to set people free from addiction. He listened intently then told me that he had never met a heroin addict who was clean. So, I took him to the Teen Challenge induction center and introduced him to Jose Marrero, one of our staff who had been delivered from heroin for years. As I drove the man home, with tears in his eyes, he gently put my hand on his face and said, "Thanks. I did not think anyone cared. That is the first time I meet someone free from heroin and now I have hope." I am glad that I took the time to give him a ride and share Christ with him. People with addiction are hurting and need someone to give of their time to enlighten them and give them hope. Who could you give of yourself to inspire an addict to get free?

Witnessing

Sharing your personal testimony is a great way to give hope to others who are caught up in an addiction. The 12th step of Alcoholics Anonymous is, "Having had a *spiritual awakening* as the result of these steps, we tried to *carry this message to alcoholics* and to practice these principles in all our affairs." Revelations 12:11 says, "They overcame him (the accuser Satan) by the blood of the Lamb (Jesus Christ) and by the word of their testimony."

Once in 1969, while on a weekend pass from Teen Challenge, I went back to my hometown and saw three of my friends standing in front of a bar. I parked and got out to talk to them. Immediately, they teased me, called me "Preacher", and asked if I wanted some drugs or a hookup with a woman. I told them that I was going to be faithful to the Lord. One of the three friends was older and a tough guy who egged the other two on to taunt me. After I witnessed to them for about 10 minutes, I drove around the corner to my apartment. When I got out of my car, another car pulled in behind me. It was the older guy. He apologized for teasing me and told me that he just wanted to see if I was for real about Christ. Then he told me that his mother had cancer and asked me to pray for her. I held his hand and prayed. I realized that he was testing me in front of the bar, and, by God's grace, I passed the test, and it had a positive impact on him. We never know the influence that we can have by sharing our testimony.

After my first quarter of Bible College, I returned to Findlay for the summer to work and save money to pay for school. I was told that a group of my old friends was partying at a house at the edge of town. I gathered up all the Bibles that I could find and drove to the house. Both of my arms were full of Bibles, so I kicked on the door. When it opened, I said, "It's Bible Study time." They were surprised to see me, and I knew that no one would oppose me because I had a tough reputation. There were about 30 people in the house and about 15 of them sat on the floor of a bedroom as I shared the word of God. They listened intently and several prayed to receive Christ into their lives. Then I started a weekly Bible study with a group of about 35 of them at a place provided by First Assembly of God Church. J.

Steve Walton and his wife, Julie, actively helped me with the group and were great supporters and encouragers. Steve is the Hancock County Treasurer in Findlay, where he has served for many years.

His father-in-law, Rev. Howard Spriggs, pastor of First Assembly of God Church, was very supportive of me. I remember telling him that I would go to bars to share Christ with my old friends and not to be concerned because I knew that I would never backslide. I had a passion for reaching my past friends with the message of hope and deliverance through Christ. I told Rev. Spriggs that he could send a deacon or someone else with me if he wanted. He let me know that he trusted me and the Christ within me. On several occasions after talking with friends about the Lord on Saturday evenings, some of them came to church with me the next morning.

Later that summer, I found out that the house where my friends were partying was shut down with yellow police tape wrapped around it because someone got stabbed by a friend of my brother Dan. I visited the guy that did the stabbing in jail. I also visited the guy he stabbed; he was nicknamed Grub, but I found out his real name is Jim Deal. He told me that he was nicknamed Grub because he scrounged around to find drugs. I lead him to Christ, gave him a Bible, and encouraged him to go into the Teen Challenge program in Harrisburg, Pennsylvania. He agreed, so I called and talked to the executive director, who had previously paid for my application for Bible College and a bus ticket to travel to school in North Dakota. He agreed to take Jim into the program and asked me to come work on the staff. I told him that I was working to save money for school. He said that he would pay for the next quarter if I would come, so Jim and I went to Harrisburg. When we arrived, the program director was packing up and told me that I was in charge. I was only 20 years old and became the resident director of the program in a mansion with 15 students. That showed how much faith the executive director had in me. I enjoyed working there and helping guys get free from their addictions. I went back to Bible College for another quarter and Jim attended the same school the next year. Recently, after 50 years, Jim called me and let me know what he was doing. He has been active in ministry and has stayed free from alcohol and drugs. I wondered about him many times in the past 50 years. Somehow, in my zeal to witness for Christ, I made a positive influence on Jim. What if I had not gone to the house or visited him after he got stabbed?

When I talked to Jim Deal recently, he reminded me that while at Harrisburg Teen Challenge, I took him and a few others to a park full of people to witness during an outdoor concert with about 6,000 people. I prayed with Jim and the others, then asked God for an opportunity to witness for Christ. Immediately after the prayer, the master of ceremonies up on the band shell informed the crowd that a band would be 30 minutes late, so if anyone would like to share something to come up and use the microphone. Some guy with a guitar went up and played a little bit, but two of his strings broke. So, I took Jim onto the stage with me and introduced him to give his testimony of how Christ had delivered him from addiction. He did a great job and the crowd seemed very receptive. Jim told me that it was the first time that he ever shared his testimony and he has continued witnessing for Christ for the past 50 years.

Here is one more example of the power of witnessing. Joe Prude worked on the staff with me at Greater Cleveland Teen Challenge and we used to spend our days-off walking around inner-city neighborhoods sharing Christ. Some days, we probably led a dozen people to Christ on our days off. Joe is now pastoring New Hope Fellowship Church in Cleveland and functions as an Apostle overseeing a group of churches and ministers. I hope you can see the importance of witnessing to others and sharing your message of hope. By giving others a glimpse of the peace and love available to them, you could genuinely make all the difference between them staying on a path to ruin or finding the glory of God. Honestly, I really could share many more stories of witnessing with wonderful results.

Coffee House Ministry

When I was the executive director at Louisiana Teen Challenge, we operated a coffee house ministry called The Caring Place, right in the middle of the French Quarter. The chairman of our board, Rev. Marvin Gorman, pastor of First Assembly of God in New Orleans, was influential in opening The Caring Place. Dozens of volunteers from the church served by witnessing on the streets in the French Quarter, praying with people, preaching or sharing their testimony inside the coffeehouse, or playing music. I wrote a street-witnessing manual and trained probably 100 people. I allowed the students at our program in Folsom, Louisiana to team up with trained mentors to witness for Christ on the streets. My philosophy was to let the new students learn evangelism soon after entering the six- to nine-month program. We never lost one student because of being exposed to the atmosphere of the French Quarter. Why wait until students left the bubble of a controlled environment to learn the importance of sharing Christ? They learned compassion for souls and became soul winners early in their recovery from addictions. If they waited until they completed the program, they may not have been equipped to witness to others once they returned home.

We also had a large coffee house ministry in Cleveland, Ohio at the Teen Challenge Induction Center. It was a large place that probably sat more than 200 people at tables to drink coffee and listen to live Christian bands, preaching, and personal testimonies. Rev. Ross raised money to purchase thousands of gospel tracks, which volunteers passed out in the community. Hundreds of people received Christ as a result. The neighborhood was tough in the inner city and a couple of times bullets were shot into our windows after hours. I used to take people with me and go into the bars to witness. I always walked in and asked the bartender if he or she minded if we passed out some religious materials. We were never refused. Some of the people from the bars would come into our coffee house and accept Christ.

Next to our coffee house was the popular Hot Dog Inn. Once, I witnessed to a guy standing outside who had been obviously drinking alcohol. He pressed a knife against my stomach and threatened me while I was witnessing to him, but I trusted God to protect me. After he told me that he was not interested in hearing about Christ, he told me that his wife was seriously ill in the hospital. I invited him into the prayer room in the basement of the coffee house and he agreed to allow me to pray for him and his wife. One of my team members was already in the prayer room on his knees with the brother of the man I had brought in. The man received Christ into his life and so did his brother. It was a great outcome for his family.

I also started a ministry for children ages four to 12 years old at the coffee house, weekly on Saturday mornings. A church donated a bus that went around picking up children so we could share God's love with them. The place was full of kids on Saturday mornings. I am sure the children's ministry reaped great benefits for the kids and the community.

Operate in the Gifts of the Holy Spirit

Many years ago, I was pastoring an Assembly of God Church in Tioga, Louisiana, and was invited by a pastor friend, Melvin Tisdale from Church on the Rock, to fly in a small airplane to attend a conference in New Orleans. At the conference, a prophet, Dr. Bill Hamon from Christian International, laid hands on me and prophesied. I did not know that any modern-day prophets existed at that time. On the flight back, I started experiencing amazing revelation and peace. After that, when visitors came to my church, I would get impressions or thoughts about them, but I did not know if it was God revealing things to me or not. I would speak publicly to couples visiting the church, telling them that I would like to talk to them briefly after the service. I shared my impressions with them, and, on every occasion, they cried and told me that the impressions were from God. Therefore, I realized that the Holy Spirit has shown me things about people. I got bolder during services and shared my words of knowledge and wisdom while I was wearing a cordless microphone. I always had the words that I recorded as I was taught by Dr. Hamon. I attended numerous conferences at Christian International where I was trained to prophesy and flow in the gifts of the Spirit. I served on prophetic teams at many conferences. I have trained many people through the years on how to hear from God and minister spiritual gifts.

While pastoring in Tioga, Louisiana I received a phone call from a young husband who was 19. He told me that his pregnant wife was in the hospital and she had some kind of toxic condition in her. The doctor did not know if she or the baby would live. Immediately, I drove to the hospital as I prayed. The husband pushed a button and informed a nurse to please let his pastor in to see his wife. While I was walking to see her, the Lord told me to tell her that she and the baby would be fine. She was lying down, ready to be wheeled into the operating room, with a doctor and a nurse standing beside her. I told her the message the Lord had given me. The doctor glared, then pulled me aside and said, "If the baby lives, it will have to be taken via Life Flight to New Orleans." I replied, "No, the mother and the baby will be fine because God told me so." When I walked into the hallway to wait, the parents of the young man and his wife were standing there beside my assistant pastor. I boldly told them what the Holy Spirit revealed to me because I knew what I had heard came from God. Perhaps about 40 minutes later, the doctor came out and told us that the mother and the baby were fine; the baby did not need to be transferred to New Orleans. The doctor asked me how I knew, and I informed him that the Holy Spirit told me. Thank God, the mother and baby were fine. I do not share this true story to make me appear super-spiritual. However, I want you to know that the gifts of the Holy Spirit are available to you also.

My brother Dan Carlin, pastor of Word Christian Fellowship in Casper, Wyoming, had a similar experience prompted by a word of knowledge that he received from the Holy Spirit that prompted a miraculous healing. Chaz Peck is a tall, muscular six-foot-six former bouncer for a strip club in Denver, Colorado, who struggled with alcohol and drug abuse. He called Dan from Wyoming Medical Center to report that he had fallen asleep outside in the cold after binging for a few days. He told Dan that the doctors were going to amputate all of his toes the next morning. Dan visited him and saw that his toes were dark black and in bad shape, so he prayed for him. When Dan was walking out of his room, he heard a voice in his head say, "Are you a man of God?" Dan answered, "Yes." Then he heard again "Are you a man of God? Go back and pray for him again. I want to heal his toes." Dan turned around, saw Chaz crying, and reassured him that he believed that God wanted to heal him.

While he was praying with him, he heard some noise in the hallway near the entrance to the room. He noticed nurses with stern faces as one of them motioned him to come to talk to her. The nurse scolded him and told him that he was giving false hope to the patient. Dan responded by saying, "You do your job and I'll do my job as a pastor to pray for him." Then he returned to Chaz and prayed again. When Dan finished, the surgeon politely informed pastor Dan that he had dealt with numerous patients through the years and was going to amputate the toes the next morning. "Toes that are that bad do not ever come back to health," the doctor said. Dan pleaded with him, "If tomorrow morning some of the blackness is gone, will you postpone the surgery?" The surgeon said it was not going to happen so he shouldn't have false hope. After the second round of discussion, the surgeon agreed that he would check the toes in the morning and, if there was any improvement, he would delay the surgery.

Dan reported that he believed in his heart that Chaz would be healed but doubted big time in his head. The next day around noon, Chaz called to inform him that he still had his toes, and they were returning to health. Dan visited him that evening and the toes were definitely healing. The surgeon said, "It is a miracle. I have never seen anything like it. It defies logic." And the nurse who had previously scolded Dan said to him, "I have learned to let pastors do their job and I'll do my job." Chaz still has all of his toes, partially thanks to a man of God who listened and obeyed. How many others could receive a miracle if more believers really listen to the Holy Spirit and acted in faith?

I also pastored at a non-denominational church in Marietta, Georgia. For years, we held a special School of the Holy Spirit on Friday evenings where we flowed in the Spirit, ministering in the gifts of the Spirit. One evening, I looked at a woman who had been attending the church for a few months, sitting in the back row. I received a word from the Holy Spirit. I told her that God showed me that her husband, who had never attended our church, would be saved, and attending church with her within a week. I boldly spoke those words on a cordless microphone in front of everyone. Sure, enough the word of knowledge came to pass, and her husband became a deacon in our church.

During a subsequent church service in Marietta, someone gave a message in tongues out loud. I cannot remember if I interpreted the message or someone else in the congregation did. A Jewish man sitting in the front row jumped up excitedly and asked to speak. He said that the message in tongues was in perfect Hebrew and the interpretation given was accurate. Our whole congregation was blessed by this experience. I could give you more examples, but hopefully you got the message that the gifts of the Holy Spirit are real and available today. Never forget:

- 2 Corinthians 3:17 "Now the Lord is the Spirit; and where the Spirit of the Lord is, there is liberty." The Spirit of the Lord gives liberty from addictions.

- Isaiah 61:1 says "The Spirit of the Lord God is upon Me, Because the Lord has anointed Me To preach good tidings to the poor; He has sent Me to heal the broken hearted, To proclaim liberty to the captives, And the opening of the prison to those who are bound."

You don't have to be a pastor in order to share your gifts. In fact, you should not hold back in fear of what others will think of your status in the church. In Luke 4:16-30, Jesus quoted Isaiah 61:1 in a synagogue and proclaimed in verse 21, "Today this Scripture was fulfilled in your hearing." The people in the synagogue were filled with wrath. They could not believe that Jesus, the son of Joseph the carpenter from Nazareth, could be anyone special or have special powers. Without the Spirit, there is only the lifeless, mechanical performance of religious duties. What do you believe? It is exciting to learn to minister spiritual gifts, which gives encouragement and comfort while building others up. Your life will be greatly enriched when you develop the gifts of the Holy Spirit and allow the life-giving river of life to flow through you. Part of the reason that I used to abuse alcohol and drugs is that I was bored, but now I am excited every day as I know that I have a purpose that is blessing me and others.

Feel free to pray this prayer for operating in the Miraculous Gifts of the Holy Spirit:

"Father God, I desire to allow the Holy Spirit to flow through me to minister life, comfort, healing, edification, and encouragement to bless others. Let the gifts of the Holy Spirit minister through me."

CHAPTER NINE
CHANGE PEOPLE, PLACES, AND THINGS

One of the first principles that people learn in treatment and recovery from addiction is the importance of changing people, places, and things to avoid internal and external triggers that could lead to relapse. Triggers are the problematic cues that lead to cravings to obtain and use your drug of choice. Your brain begins to expect a certain drug when a trigger is present through the people, places, and things associated with substance abuse. These factors you experience every day play a vital role in encouraging or discouraging substance use, no matter the stage of addiction or recovery. If you want to remain addiction-free, you must make some changes to the people, places, and things with which you normally engage. It is not enough to limit the negative elements in your life. You must actively seek out positive people, experiences, and activities that will promote and enhance recovery.

People

People triggers can include a wide range of individuals from your past and present, such as people that you drank alcohol or used drugs with; family members; dealers that you bought drugs from; current or former romantic partners; coworkers, etc. People triggers do not just include those you got high with. They can also be the important people in your life who are capable of pushing your buttons to create strong emotional responses. Through engaging different positive people in new situations, your brain can build associations to replace the old triggers with healthy stimuli. Reconnecting with friends and family members with whom you have positive and supportive relationships can be very beneficial for sobriety.

I Corinthians 15:33 says, "Do not be deceived: Evil company corrupts good habits." Psalm 1:1 states, "Blessed is the man who walks not in the counsel of the ungodly, nor stands in the path of sinners, nor sits in the seat of the scornful."

The people we hang out with really do affect us in life. If we socialize with drug or alcohol abusers, most likely we will do what they do. We can be influenced by those we spent time with. And we can also influence some people in positive ways. We must set healthy boundaries and wisely choose who we associate with. Whose approval is more important to you—other people's or God's?

When I was a student in Bible college in North Dakota, I used to accompany Prof. Paul Davidson on long walks in often sub-zero weather. I dislike cold weather, but I chose to take advantage of the opportunity to gain the wisdom he shared during our discipling walks. Those walks with Prof. Davidson were very valuable to my development and learning. As Proverbs 13:20 says, "He who walks with wise men will be wise, but the companion of fools will be destroyed."

Places

Many of the places that can trigger you are obvious, such as a certain bar where you used to drink heavily. There is no completely accurate way to predict all triggers. Any location that reminds you of substance abuse should be avoided if at all possible. Think before you go out somewhere if the spot you are planning to go could be a trigger to avoid.

If it is, think of an alternative place to spend your time. If you are in recovery from alcohol or drugs and get invited to a wedding reception where alcohol or drugs may be available, then take someone with you that will encourage you in sobriety or just congratulate the bride and groom and leave.

Things

There is a long list of things that can create cravings, ranging from items, events, words, and sensations. Be aware of potential dangers such as money in your pocket, paydays, drug paraphernalia (straws, needles, smells, pill bottles, pipes), parties, holidays, feelings (anxiety, depression, stress, boredom, anger, loneliness), anniversaries, certain kinds of music, and physical pain, etc. They need to be evaluated for potential triggers. Make wise choices to avoid things that could trigger a relapse. The things that we allow in our lives can affect us positively or negatively.

Re-engaging in old healthy hobbies you once enjoyed, like playing music, hiking, or sports is great to do. For instance, music can create a great mood so be mindful of what you listen to. Ecclesiastes 7:5 says, "It is better to hear the rebuke of the wise, than for a man to hear the song of fools." Psalm 32:7 adds, "You (God) are my hiding place; You shall preserve me from trouble; You shall surround me with songs of deliverance." Do not listen to "crying in your beer" songs that can be depressing; instead, listen to praise and worship music that feeds your soul with a positive message and helps you keep your mind on the Lord.

Biblical Exhortation to Put off / Put on

People often fail to change because they try to adapt solely by quitting bad habits. However, a change that lasts will not take place until you replace bad habits with good habits. The Bible has much to say about the importance of *putting off* and *putting on* so we can live fulfilled lives. Ephesians 4:22-32 says, "Put off, concerning your former conduct, the old man which grows corrupt according to the deceitful lusts and be renewed in the spirit of your mind, and that you put on the new man which was created according to God, in righteousness and true holiness. Therefore, putting away lying, each one speaks truth with his neighbor, for we are members of one another. Be angry, and do not sin: do not let the sun go down on your wrath, nor give place to the devil. Let him who stole steal no longer, but rather let him labor, working with his hands what is good, that he may have something to give him who has need. Let no corrupt communication proceed out of your mouth, but what is good for necessary edification, that it may impart grace to the hearers. And do not grieve the Holy Spirit of God, by whom you were sealed for the day of redemption. Let all bitterness, wrath, anger, clamor, and evil speaking be put away from you, with all malice. And be kind to one another, tender-hearted, forgiving one another, just as God in Christ also forgave you."

We see from Scriptures in Ephesians and Colossians that we are exhorted to:

Put off	**Put on**
Former conduct of the old man. Ephesians 4:22 Colossians 3:9	Put on the new man. Ephesians 4:24 Colossians 3:10
Put off stealing. Ephesians 4:28	Labor, working with hands, and giving to those in need. Ephesians 4:28
Corrupt communication. Ephesians 4:29	Speak what is good to edification and imparting grace. Ephesians 4:29, Colossians 3:16

Bitterness, wrath, anger clamor, evil speaking, and malice. Ephesians 4:31 Anger, wrath, malice, blasphemy, filthy language. Colossians 3:8	Be kind, tender-hearted, and forgiving. Ephesians 4:32 Tender mercies, kindness, humility, meekness, long suffering, bearing with one another, forgiving. Colossians 3: 12-13
Fornication, uncleanness, passion, evil desire, covetousness which is idolatry. Colossians 3:3:3	
Lying. Ephesians 4:25 & Colossians 3:9	Speak truth. Ephesians 4:25
	Love. Colossians 3:14
	The whole armor of God. Ephesians 6:11

There are numerous Bible verses regarding putting off and putting on. This principle of replacement is very important to understand and practice for all Christians, but especially for those desiring to overcome addictions or some other life-controlling problem. We are to put off our former addictive behavior, renew our minds, and put on the new way of life. The process of change takes more than simply confessing to God or others our regrets or asking for forgiveness.

For instance, it is not enough for a habitual thief to tell God he is sorry every time he steals. For true change to take place, new behavior must be demonstrated. The thief changes his lifestyle by laboring in good work with his hands and giving to others in need. This shows evidence that the former thief has truly made a positive change in his life. Simply apologizing or saying I am sorry is not adequate. In most cases, a lifestyle change is needed to overcome the negative behavior that traps people in addiction. What changes can you make to prove that you really are changing for the better? Take responsibility and truly change with God's help; it is truly possible to replace bad habits with good habits with the highest power working in your life.

I Corinthians 6:9-11 gives me hope that people do and can change. It says, "Do you not know that the unrighteous will not inherit the kingdom of God? Do not be deceived. Neither fornicators, nor idolaters, nor adulterers, nor homosexuals, nor sodomites, nor thieves, nor covetous, nor drunkards, nor revilers, nor extortioners will inherit the kingdom of God. And such were some of you. But you were washed, but you were sanctified, but you were justified in the name of the Lord Jesus and by the Spirit of our God." Personally, I am guilty of many of the negative behaviors mentioned, but I have found grace to be sanctified or set apart and justified by the power of Jesus Christ and the Holy Spirit.

I Peter 2:9-10 says, "But you are a chosen generation, a royal priesthood, a holy nation, His own special people, that you may proclaim the praises of Him who called you out of darkness into His marvelous light; who once were not a people but are now the people of God, who had not obtained mercy but now have obtained mercy." Addiction is part of the darkness, but God's marvelous light and mercy are available to free whoever will hear and respond to His call. I praise God for freeing me and allowing me to see thousands of others set free. There is a positive addiction mentioned in I Corinthians 16:15 regarding believers that have addicted themselves to the ministry of the saints.

Making radical positive changes can be challenging, but important. After I graduated from the Teen Challenge programs, I went straight to Bible college and grew stronger in the Lord. Therefore, I realized that other graduates from Teen Challenge programs could also benefit from going to a good Bible college. Bible college provides an environment that helps ex-addicts grow in faith. While working at Greater Cleveland Teen Challenge, my father-in-law, Dr. Harry Hall, a medical doctor, was a board member. I told him that if our graduates attended Bible college for a year, it would solidify their faith. Many of the graduates came from environments where drug addicts were still actively using. Dr. Hall told me, "Buff, if any Teen Challenge graduates desire to go to Bible college, I will pay for them to go for a year." So, I made trips from Ohio to North Dakota to drive graduates to the same Bible college that I attended. We had a 15-passenger van that we would fill up with graduates and their luggage. Many of the graduates met their future wives in Bible college and entered the ministry of the gospel.

Sometimes I think of the thousands of addicts and other people that have probably found new, fulfilling lives, because of the influence of these former addicts that graduated from Teen Challenge, attended Bible college, and have dedicated their lives to helping others. God only knows the fruitfulness of Dr. Hall's generosity. I remain grateful for God's amazing grace and blessings. One of the former Teen Challenge graduates found a wife in Bible college and started a successful business.

What changes in people, places, and things are you willing to make for sobriety? We all have gifts, talents, and anointing that can blossom in the right atmosphere.

CHAPTER TEN
BEWARE OF BLASTS FROM THE PAST

After you make a commitment to avoid alcohol and drugs, things from your past will start to blast you. Trust me, I've been there. Soon after my exorcism and giving my life to the Lord, an ex-girlfriend who moved to a large city in Ohio called me and asked me to come to live with her. She told me that she had become a high-class prostitute with wealthy clients. She begged me to move in with her and told me that I would not have to work because she would take care of me and would buy me all the alcohol and drugs I wanted. I turned down her offer because I realized that Satan was using her to tempt me back into my alcohol and drug lifestyle. If she had asked me a few weeks earlier, I probably would have gone. That blast from my recent past would have led me back to a life of alcohol, drugs, and probably violence.

A year or so after I had decided to follow Jesus, I was home visiting my mother when a police officer and an FBI agent came to my mother's house to arrest me. My mother shouted, "Buff has changed. He graduated from a Teen Challenge program and has been attending Bible college. Please don't arrest him." At the police station, they asked me about a crime that I was involved with about two years prior. A friend had stolen a check from an old lady; another friend signed the check and I drove to a bank drive-through and cashed the check. I admitted that I was guilty. The FBI agent said that the signature on the check was not mine and wanted to know whose it was. I told him I knew but would not rat or snitch on anyone. They agreed not to lock me in jail if I would agree to go to the FBI office in Toledo, Ohio the next day, and I promised that I would.

I asked if he would give me a couple of days to find the other two guys and talk to them to see if they would turn themselves in. I also asked what they intended to do to us. The FBI agent said that if we admitted to the crime and paid the money back, then he would let us go. So, I talked to the two friends and they agreed to turn themselves in with me at the FBI office. Praise God, not one of us served jail time for the whole incident. I had asked my pastor, Rev. Spriggs at First Assembly of God Church in Findlay, to pray for me about the situation. And God delivered me from that blast from the past or I would have started my prison ministry earlier than I did!

Another brief blast from the past popped up on my first day at Bible college in January 1970. The college was located in an old hospital building. When I arrived on the 4th floor with my suitcase, there were two guys boxing with gloves with a group of students watching. I watched for about five minutes and thought to myself, "I could knock both of them out." Then I realized that it was my old pride encouraging me to box to get recognition. I realized that I if had offered to spar that I would be known for fighting again, be challenged by others to box, and slip back into my old identity. Thank God, He helped me to think it through and avoid it.

Another blast from my past came when I started dating my first wife, who has since passed away. I remember picking her up and hesitating to open the passenger car door for her. Even though I was 100 miles away from my hometown and old friends, I could hear them in my mind saying, "Only wimps open car doors for females." A few years earlier, while in Bible college, I refused to offer this courtesy for girls due to that old mindset. However, I overcame those negative thoughts and opened the door for my soon wife-to-be. Unfortunately, she died at an early age about eight years after our wedding.

Many addicts are controlled by things that are still in their heads that can blast them into doing good things. 2 Corinthians 10:4-5 says, "For the weapons of our warfare are not carnal but mighty in God for pulling down strongholds. Casting down arguments and every high thing that exalts itself against the knowledge of God, bringing every thought into captivity to the obedience of Christ." Be careful not to allow any unhealthy or wrong thinking to influence your thoughts and actions. Probably because I used to hang out with friends that were addicts, and often criminals, my thinking was distorted. I remember eating at fancy restaurants and telling my wife on several occasions that other diners thought they were better than me. Where did those thoughts come from?

During my last quarter of Bible college, I received another blast that I thought could not affect me anymore. During the last few days of the term, I was studying for final exams in my room as two other students aggravated me by bouncing a basketball on my door. When I opened the door to ask them to quit, they tried to get me to fight them. My mind thought, "They don't realize who they are messing with, because I could easily throw them out of the 4th-floor window." I felt like saying, if it was not for Jesus, I would clean their clocks, but I refrained. Thankfully, I managed to avoid a physical fight.

On my last day of Bible college in December 1970, I ended up sitting right beside both of them in the last row during chapel. The temperature was probably below zero there in North Dakota. The main instigator of the two was sitting beside me and reached behind me and opened the window about six inches. It was freezing cold, so I shut the window. Then he opened it again. Then I snapped and said, "Both of you outside after chapel. I am going to beat the crap out of both of you." I said it, meant it, and was committed to doing it. Believe me, I was not afraid of them at all. Then the chapel leader announced that we were going to partake of the holy communion, and I knew that I was supposed to check out my heart in obedience to the Lord. I did not want to back down from the two students and wrestled with the situation in my mind. God impressed me strongly to apologize and take communion. I did not want to miss out on hurting those guys, but my desire to please God was more powerful. So, I humbled myself and apologized, they probably thought I was afraid, but I wasn't. I realized that this blast could have affected my whole life in a negative way.

Blasts from the past will attack us, but we do not need to succumb to them. As 1 Corinthians 10:13 says, "No temptation has overtaken you except such as is common to man; but God is faithful, who will not allow you to be tempted beyond what you are able, but with the temptation will also make the way of escape, that you may be able to bear it." The same God that delivered me from addictions, temptations, and wrong mindsets is available for anyone that will call upon and trust Him. Whatever blast comes, we can find a way to escape so we can bear it.

Because I used to stay out nights partying, slept through many of my high school classes, and did not complete homework assignments, I could not write very well. Therefore, I struggled to complete writing assignments while attending college to earn a BA in Social Service. My past partying and laziness caught up to me and blasted me with thoughts that I would never graduate from college. I felt like giving up due to the bombardment of discouraging thoughts. However, I hired an English teacher to tutor me and I managed to learn to write well enough to graduate. Sometimes your past comes back to haunt you in ways that you cannot even imagine.

LSD flashbacks unexpectedly happened to me on and off for about five years after I stopped using it. For instance, while in bed lying on my back awake, I would suddenly see huge butterflies flying above me for a few minutes. I realized what I was seeing were hallucinations and were not real.

A year or two after I committed my life to Jesus Christ, I drove into my hometown to visit. I stopped by a gas station where my brother Dan had been working, but he was not there. The guy that was working told me that my brother just had stopped by and reported that he had been beaten up by some guys at the Pub, a bar catering to college students. He was headed to the Paradise, a bar across the street from the Pub, to round up friends to go into the Pub to beat up the guys that jumped him. I immediately drove to the Pub and got there just as my brother arrived at the front door with his friends. Dan's friends were tough guys who may have had knives or other weapons on them. I jumped out of my car while yelling stop, and fortunately, my brother and his friends listened to me. I believe that God divinely had me in town just at the right moment to prevent bloodshed. I was unexpectedly confronted with a situation that was a blast from my past. Of course, it was natural for me to want to fight for my brother and old friends. And I felt obligated to stand with my brother. If I had arrived seconds later, who knows how many would have been hurt and arrested, perhaps even me. The Lord protected me again from a blast from the past. Sometimes unexpected blasts confront us, but God will make a way of escape.

CHAPTER ELEVEN
THE JESUS FACTOR: BUT GOD

I have referred to the Jesus Factor as the reason for the high success rate in Teen Challenge programs for overcoming addictions and other life-controlling problems. The addictions treatment and recovery fields have gone through many changes as new theories and practices have emerged with promising best and evidence-based practices. Many devoted practitioners have contributed greatly to our present-day understanding of what works and does not work in helping people recover from addictive behaviors. Neuroscience has identified how brain chemistry is affected by substances ingested into our bodies that reach the brain and often restructure the chemical interaction, making it difficult to function properly. That process makes it especially difficult to abstain from a drug of choice that has been abused.

The two major forms of treatment for substance abuse in the secular arena are psychosocial treatments and pharmacological treatments. They both have their strengths and limitations, especially when used alone. No particular counseling technique has consistently emerged as the more superior option. No single treatment model is effective for all individuals. Probably more than 90 percent of all the substance abuse treatment programs in America emphasizes the importance of developing spirituality. However, most seem not to promote or even acknowledge Jesus Christ in an effort to be politically correct or spiritually open and to not offend anyone that believes in anything else.

In the 1970s, when I was involved in prison ministry, I met the executive director of addiction treatment programs in the greater Cleveland area whose programs included at least one methadone clinic, outpatient treatment programs, and residential treatment programs. He had medical and mental health staff and received millions of federal, state, county, and probably city public funds to treat addictions. He rode with me and a Mennonite minister to prison and spent the day with us. During lunch in the staff lunchroom, I asked him about the success rate of his programs. He beat around the bush and did not really answer my questions. So, I asked him a direct question: "Do you know of one heroin addict who has been cured in the five years that you have been the executive director of the treatment programs?" He said, "No." I told him that I could introduce him to dozens of former heroin addicts that have been clean for years in the Cleveland area after graduating from the Greater Cleveland Teen Challenge. I told him that they would submit to urine drug screens as proof. He replied, "That is bullsh--." He did not believe me.

The Mennonite minister knew the man well and also was well acquainted with Teen Challenge, so he told him that what I said was true. He also knew dozens of those young recovered heroin addicts. Many addiction treatment professionals are unfamiliar with the Jesus factor, which is the highest power that actually works successfully in recovery from addictions. On the positive side, I have personally met probably 100 or more addicts over many years who have overcome their past addictions by participating in treatment programs that did not promote or encourage belief in Jesus Christ. There are successful, secular addiction treatment programs in the world. However, I believe that many more addicts could achieve recovery through Christ, who is greater than any other higher power.

Statistically, about 1 out of every 10 American adults are dependent upon alcohol and/or drugs, whether they abuse illegal drugs or prescription medications. Alcohol and drug-use disorders affect people from all backgrounds and vocations. Almost everyone either has a family member, friend, colleague, neighbor, co-worker, or acquaintance who has struggled or is struggling with addiction issues and the devastating effects on their lives and those close to them. The fall-out from addictions costs America untold millions of dollars in lost productivity, medical expenses, thefts, accidents, and prosecuting and incarcerating criminals that have committed crimes under the influence of alcohol or drugs. Add to that the emotional pain, violence, verbal and physical abuse, and the breakup of families due to life-controlling addictions, and it easy to see and feel the impact on our society as a whole.

The war on drugs in America has not been successful in limiting the flow of illicit drugs from entering our country. Those drugs make it to communities large and small throughout our country. Illicit drugs and prescription drugs are bought and sold in most, if not all, cities and towns. Is there a way to stop most of this from happening? It is a very inexpensive answer. If there was no demand for drugs or, in other words, no one purchasing them, then the illegal market of drug traffickers would have no one to sell them to. Most campaigns to stop or significantly slow down the illegal sales of drugs have failed miserably. As long as a significant percentage of people choose to "get high" on drugs and spend money to support their habits, there will always be drug sales.

What could happen if Christian believers, especially the ones that have overcome addiction, shared the positive news about Christ's power to free people from addiction? It is time for true believers to rise up and share the good news of the gospel. Then people would be less likely to fall into the deceitful trap of pharmakeia or need to be told Biblical advice on how to get free through Jesus Christ. Do you believe that the Bible has knowledge that can truly help people recover from addictions? Are you ready for a spiritual awakening?

But God

What does *But God* mean? The word "but" in Scripture often introduces the message of the gracious and compassionate intervention of God. This simple term captures the nature of our God. God redeems our lives from destruction as written in Psalm 103:4. No matter how bad or far we have gone in addiction, God can make all things new as indicated in 2 Corinthians 5:17. All may seem lost and then we hear, "but God and He intervenes. There seemed to be no way, but God made a way for the children of Israel to pass through the red sea and He will provide a way for us if we call upon Him."

Genesis 37-50 tells the story of Joseph, who was betrayed by his jealous brothers, thrown in a pit, sold as a slave, put in prison for a crime he did not commit, and eventually became the governor of Egypt. Joseph told his brothers in Genesis 45:7, "God sent me before you to preserve a posterity for you in the earth, and to save your lives by a great deliverance. So now it was not you who sent me here, but God." And in Genesis 50:20 he adds, "But as for you, you meant evil against me, but God meant it for good, in order to bring it about as it is this day, to save many people alive."

Perhaps through my mother's prayers, God allowed me to go through alcohol and drug problems. Then he delivered me and turned my life around so that I could save many people from addiction problems through the knowledge and power of God. There are very many scriptures that share the *But God* concept:

- Romans 5:8 – "But God demonstrates His own love toward us, in that while we were still sinners Christ died for us."

- Ephesians 2:4 – "But God, who is rich in mercy, because of His great love with which He loved us, even when we were dead in trespasses, made us alive together with Christ (by grace you have been saved)."

- 1 Corinthians 10:13 - "No temptation has overtaken you except such as is common to man; but God is faithful, who will not allow you to be tempted beyond what you are able, but with the temptation will also make the way of escape, that you may be able to bear it."

- Psalm 49:15 – "But God will redeem my soul from the power

of the grave."

Think of how many addicts have overdosed and narrowly escaped death. I have met hundreds that have survived overdoses. But I also know of hundreds that have died from overdoses. We should be using every tool available to try to save more lives, including the Word and power of God.

CHAPTER TWELVE
HOPE FOR A BETTER FUTURE

I have come a long way from abusing alcohol and drugs, criminal behavior, and being judged as incorrigible, delinquent, and unruly with a bad reputation for fighting and rebellion. Around 1972, I was invited to speak at a civic group in my hometown. Judge Robert Payne, a juvenile judge that knew me well from my earlier life of appearing before him, introduced me. "There is a difference between night and day in this young man," he said. It gave me a sense of accomplishment that I was able to make a dramatic change in my life with God's help. Allen Davis was my attorney for some of my cases in the past and he became the next Juvenile Court Judge after Judge Payne. Several times through the years I visited with Judge Davis in his chambers when I was back in Findlay. He was always gracious to me and recognized that I truly changed to become a productive citizen.

I served as an assistant pastor in two churches in Ohio (Christian Centre Foursquare Church in Cleveland and Kettering Assembly of God in Kettering) after I resigned from Greater Cleveland Teen Challenge to pursue pastoral ministry. I have planted three churches that I have pastored. I attended a pastor's meeting in Akron, Ohio where my childhood pastor, Carl Malz, was the speaker. He told me that when he pastored First Assembly of God in Findlay, he called a special board meeting to decide what to do with the Carlin boys. Apparently, my brothers and I were that far on the wild side. However, we are now all involved in ministry either pastoring, playing music on praise and worship teams, teaching Sunday School classes, Christian counseling, or coaching at a Christian high school.

Maybe leopards cannot change their spots, but the greatest higher power in the universe has changed me, my brothers, and millions of others. I have had the privilege of preaching chapel services to professional athletes in the NFL and MLB. I have preached the gospel in foreign countries, including for soldiers at an army base in Russia. With the anointing of the Holy Spirit, I have helped marriages to be healed and clients to overcome mental health problems. Life is a joy and very fulfilling for me. Addiction can be overcome, and a better life is really possible. On Sept. 13, 2007, the mayor of my hometown honored my brothers and me by giving each of us a key to the city and proclaiming that day as "Carlin Brothers' Day." Who would have thought that an incorrigible alcohol and drug abuser like me would receive such an honor in a city where I committed many crimes? A higher power than me made it possible. You can have a brighter future also. Proverbs 14:12 says "There is a way that seems right to a man, but its end is the way of death." Choose life. Jesus said in John 14:6 "I am the way, the truth, and the life. No one comes to the Father except through me."

No matter what the addiction or life-controlling problem, you can break free and enjoy an abundant life. Many do not believe that addictions can be broken, but I assure you that it is more than possible. As Philippians 4:13 says, "I can do all things through Christ who strengthens me." And Jesus said in Luke 18:27, "The things which are impossible with men are possible with God." To recover from addiction, you have to believe it's possible and step out in faith on a wonderful journey. The principles that I have shared in this book will put you on a path that will free you today and forever. In Jeremiah 29:11, it says, "For I know the thoughts that I think toward you, says the Lord, thoughts of peace and not of evil, to give you a future and a hope."

Some think that there is no or very little hope that people with addictions can change. Remember, statistically most addicts recover without formal treatment, according to multiple research studies. You, your loved ones, friends, and coworkers can experience supernatural recovery. I shared how Teen Challenge has had tremendous success in helping addicts become free from addictions. Technically, Teen Challenge programs are not treatment programs; they simply provide an atmosphere where addicts learn about Jesus Christ as the highest power. Teen Challenges do not educate the students in the programs about addiction causes or effects, relapse prevention strategies, statistics regarding alcohol and drug problems, or new methods or medications to treat addiction. They do not provide group therapy sessions or schedule individual counseling sessions with students. However, the staff are available to provide Biblical guidance, prayer, and discipling. The staff members provide love and positive role modeling. They focus on the answer, which is faith in the grace of Jesus Christ. As revealed in Hebrews 13:8, "Jesus Christ is the same yesterday, today, and forever." He has been freeing addicts for years, is still doing it, and will continue to do it.

While working at Greater Cleveland Teen Challenge, I probably appeared in court hundreds of times to advocate for addicts to be permitted to participate in the program instead of being sent to prison. I often met with attorneys in a judge's chambers prior to the hearings and, as a result, many young people were allowed to come into the Teen Challenge program. One young man who had an addiction and sold drugs was Jim Harman, whom I advocated for in 1973. He received mercy and entered our program. Jim had a powerful transformation through Jesus Christ and has never abused or sold drugs again. His family appreciated the wonderful change in Jim so much that they became active supporters of the program. Jim's father, Robert Harman joined the board of Greater Cleveland Teen Challenge and built a chapel on the property before retiring. Nowadays, Jim is serving on the board supporting young men to be discipled and grow in Christ. Jim's brother, Dr. Robert Harman, has directed several Teen Challenge programs. Currently, Dr. Harman is the executive director of the Greater Piedmont Teen Challenge in Greensboro, North Carolina. His wife, Deborah, is also working there as a business manager with him. The Harman family dedicated themselves to the ministry of Teen Challenge, which started with prayer and concern for Jim and the powerful changes observed in his life.

I have been volunteering one day per month at Greater Piedmont Teen Challenge for more than seven years, during which time I preach chapel and facilitate a group-therapy session with the students. My courtroom experiences since turning my life over to Christ has made a positive impact on many addicts and their families. Who could have imagined that someone with my tainted past in the criminal justice system could get turned around and bless others? There is hope that becomes reality in changing lives for the better.

I have shared my thesis with you on why I believe deeply in supernatural recovery. Although there are many paths to recovery, Jesus Christ is higher than all others and there is no other God that can deliver as completely as Him with many benefits. Now you know my story and why I believe as I do. What do you believe? Biblical truths and promises are available for everyone that will believe. A wonderful, abundant life is within reach if we will call upon the Lord. The boredom that caused me to use alcohol and drugs does not exist in my life anymore. Life is now full of excitement and fulfillment for me.

I want you to know that I am not against addicts getting treatment. I am an addiction therapist and have provided individual and group therapy treatment for many years. I was an addiction therapist with the Department of Veterans Affairs, Wyoming Recovery, Addiction Recovery Medical Services (where Suboxone and Methadone are administered), and several other programs. Some clients can benefit from medical detoxification and other treatment interventions. However, I encourage clients to consider supernatural recovery through Jesus Christ to enhance treatment outcomes if they participate in treatment since it enhances traditional programs so powerfully.

The Bible is replete with verses about hope. Take time to read and meditate on them and you will be filled with hope and peace.

No matter what addiction or related issues you face, God will surely deliver you and give you victory. Hebrews 11:1-2 says, "Now faith is the substance of things hoped for, the evidence of things not seen. For by it the elders obtained a good testimony." When we have faith based on hope in Christ, we will obtain a good testimony. Our past does not need to define our future. The evidence of our faith will be manifest if we diligently hope to obtain the promises of God. According to Hebrews 6: 18-19, "It is impossible for God to lie, we might have strong consolation who have fled for refuge to lay hold of the hope set before us. This hope we have as an anchor of the soul." Other scriptural references to hope include: Romans 15:13, I Thessalonians 5:8, Ephesians 1:18, Philippians 3:6 and 33, I Peter 1:33, Psalm 146:5, 43:5, 119:81, and Isaiah 40:31.

God told Joshua as recorded in Joshua: 1, "Every place that the sole of your foot will tread upon I have given you." By faith, I apply it to my life as meaning wherever I go, God is with me and His light within me will dispel or push back the darkness, so I walk with confidence. As God also told Joshua in chapter one: be strong and courageous, do not be afraid or dismayed, for God is with you wherever you go, and that He would never leave him or forsake him. You can walk through life with confidence, knowing that as Romans 8:37-39 tells us, "Yet in all these things we are more than conquerors through Him who loved us. For I am persuaded that neither death nor life, nor angels nor principalities nor powers, nor things present, nor things to come, nor height nor depth, nor any other created thing, shall be able to separate us from the life of God which is in Christ Jesus our Lord." If God be for us, who can be against us?

The greatest and highest power in the universe loves us all and is ready, willing, and able to come into our lives upon invitation. Jesus said in Revelations 3:20, "Behold, I stand at the door and knock, if anyone hears My voice and opens the door, I will come into him and dine with him, and he with Me." I encourage you to open your heart to Jesus Christ and allow Him to come in. If you apply the strategies that I shared in this book, you will be very blessed. Recovery from addictions is totally possible.

Ephesians 3:20 tells us, "Now to Him who is able to do

exceedingly abundantly above all that we ask or think, according to the power that works in us." We all have our own stories. How will your story end? I have told you my story and hope that in some way it has inspired you to invite the greater than a higher power to come into your life.

I regret many of the things that I have done, but I know that I have been forgiven and am now enjoying an abundant life helping others find hope. Now I do not fear death and am ready for it whenever it may happen. Ecclesiastes 7:1 says, "A good name is better than precious ointment, and the day of death than the day of one's birth." I believe I have a good name now because of Christ in my life. We can change and leave a good legacy. The choice is ours of how we shall live. Supernatural recovery from addiction is available yesterday, today, and forever.

REFERENCES/BIBLIOGRAPHY

Chapter Two

1. Davies, T. Witton, "Witch, Witchcraft," (Eds.) James Orr, et al., *The International Standard Bible Encyclopedia*, (Chicago: The Howard-Severance Company, 1915), p. 3097.

2. Nemu, Danny, "Getting High with the Most High: Drugs in the Bible," (*Ancient Origins*, 27 February 2018), https://www.ancient-origins.net/history-ancient-traditions/getting-high-most-high-drugs-bible-009665

3. Orem, Robert A, Jr., *Pharmakia: The Biblical View of Drug Use*, (Mount Airy, NC: Robert Orem Publisher, 2019),

4. Joyner, Rick, *Overcoming Witchcraft*, (Charlotte, NC: Morningstar Publications, 1996), p. 7.

5. https://www.whatchristianswanttoknow.com/what-does-the-bible-say-about-drugs/#ixzz6TLvB45Nt

6. Swanson, James. Dictionary of Biblical Languages with Semantic Domains: Greek (New Testament). Oak Harbor: Logos Research Systems, Inc., 1997.

7. Zodhiates, Spiros. The Complete Word Study Dictionary: New Testament. Chattanooga, TN: AMG Publishers, 2000.

8. Louw, Johannes P., and Eugene Albert Nida. Greek-English Lexicon of the New Testament: Based on Semantic Domains. New York: United Bible Societies, 1996.

9. Diagnostic and Statistical Manual of Mental Disorders, 5th Edition 2013

by American Psychiatric Association: DSM-5

10. The Biology of Desire: Why Addiction Is Not a Disease by Marc Lewis Hardcover, 256 pages, July 14, 2015 by Public Affairs ISBN 1610394372 (ISBN13: 9781610394376)

11. Lance Dodes M.D. Is Addiction Really a Disease? Psychology Today posted Dec. 17, 2011. https://www.psychologytoday.com/us/experts/lance-dodes-md

12. Tim Holden, MMed (Psych), Psychiatrist and assistant professor CMAJ. 2012 Apr 3; 184(6): 679.doi: 10.1503/cmaj.112-2033

13. Vine's Expository Dictionary

14. Strong's Exhaustive Concordance

Chapter Five

1. Winick C. Maturing out of narcotic addiction. Bulletin on Narcotics, January/March 1962;1–7. 7.

2. Dawson DA, Grant BF, Stinson FS, Chou PS. Maturing out of alcohol dependence: the impact of transitional life events. J Stud Alcohol. 2006;67 (2):195–203.

3. Jochman KA, Fromme K. Maturing out of substance use: the other side of etiology. In: Scheier LM, editor. Handbook of Drug Use Etiology: Theory, Methods, and Empirical Findings. Washington, DC: American Psychological Association; 2009.

4. Labouvie E. Maturing out of substance use: selection and self-correction. J Drug Issues. 1996;26(2):457–476.

5. Littlefield AK, Sher KJ, Wood PK. Is "maturing out" of problematic alcohol involvement related to personality change? J Abnormal Psychology. 2009;118(2):360–374.

6. Maddux JF, Desmond DP. New light on the maturing out hypothesis in opioid dependence. Bulletin on Narcotics. 1980;32(1):15–25.

7. Biernacki, Patrick; 1986. Pathways from Heroin Addiction. Recovery without treatment. Philadelphia, Temple University Press.

8. Anglin, Douglas M. et ai, 1986, An Empirical Study of Maturing Out: Conditional Factors. International Journal of Addictions, 21(2), 1986,

pp. 233 - 246.

9. Waldorf, D.; 1973. Rock bottom. Careers in Dope. Prentice Hall Inc. Englewood Cliffs. N.J. Chapter 9. Waldorf, D. and lliemacki, P.; 1981. The Natural Recovery from Opiate Addiction. Journal of Drug Issues. 1981. (Winter) Vol. II. no.1. pp. 61 - 74. See further: Brill; 1974, Colemann; 1978.

10. Snow, M., 1973, Maturing Out of Narcotic Addiction in New York City, The Inlerna-1i00wl Journal of the Addie/iolls, 8(6), pp. 921 - 938.

11. Waldorf, Dan and Diernacki, Patrick, 1979, The Natural Recovery from Opiate Addiction, Some preliminary findings, Journal of Drug Issues 1981. (winter) pp, 61 -74, Waldorf, Dan, 1983, Natural Recovery from Opiate Addiction: Some social-psychological processes of untreated recovery, Journal of Drug issues, Spring, pp. 237 -280

12. Waldorf, Dan (1983). Natural recovery from opiate addiction: Some social-psychological processes of untreated recovery. *Journal of Drug Issues, 13* (Spring), *237-280.*

13. Waldorf, Dan & Biernacki, Patrick (1981). The natural recovery from opiate addiction. Some preliminary findings. *Journal of Drug Issues, 11*(Winter), *61-74.*

14. Winick, Charles (1962). Maturing out of narcotic addiction. *Bulletin on Narcotics, January/March*, 1-7.

15. Maturing Out - The Stanton Peele Addiction Website peele.net/lib/maturingout.html

16. LABOUVIE, E. Maturing out of substance use: Selection and self-correction. Journal of Drug Issues 26:457–476, 1996.

17. Winick C. (1962). "Maturing Out of Narcotic Addiction," Bulletin on Narcotics., 14, 1-7. http://www.unodc.org/unodc/en/data-and-analysis/bulletin/bulletin_1962-01-01_1_page002.html

18. https://peele.net/lib/maturingout.html

19. https://www.ncbi.nlm.nih.gov/pmc/articles/PMC6601682/

7. Smart, Reginald 1975- "Spontaneous recovery in alcoholics: a review and analysis of available 1976 research." *Drug and Alcohol Dependence. 1 (4)* The review of the studies presented here documents the fact that significant numbers of heroin addicts naturally recover from their addiction without treatment intervention.

Chapter Seven

Grace, The Power of the Gospel by Andrew Wommack, 2007, Published by Harrison House Publishers

Destined to Reign by Joseph Prince, 2007, Published by Harrison House Publishers

ADDITIONAL RESOURCES

1. Access the free resources that accompany this book at: ecarecounseling.com or greaterthanahigherpower.com

2. Andrew Wommack Ministries https://www.awmi.net/about-us/demo/#free_downloads_section

3. Free Discipleship Evangelism course download

4. https://sidroth.org/ Sid Roth's It's Supernatural (704) 943-6500

5. Sid Roth is the host of It's Supernatural television, which features guests who have experienced extraordinary healings, miracles, and personal encounters with God.

6. Christ For All Nations https://cfan.org/ Conducts healing and evangelism crusades around the world

7. https://www.cai.org/health-healing/evangelists Christian Assemblies International share stories of healing evangelists

8. https://www.jonasclark.com/jack-coe-voice-of-healing-evangelist/

9. https://www.charismanews.com/opinion/48798-the-healing-miracles-preacher

10. https://www.honeylake.clinic/mental_heath/treatment Christian addiction and mental health treatment center (877) 973-9246

11. https://www.cookerevivals.org/ (844) 447-4567

12. https://www.generals.org   Generals International is a prayer-based organization founded by Mike and Cindy Jacobs in 1985 that exists for the purpose of changing lives and transforming nations. We are passionate about the message that God cares about every individual, He cares about every nation, and He still speaks to us today. Out of that passion, we develop resources and events to equip believers in spiritual warfare, intercession, and the prophetic.

13. Adult & Teen Challenge https://teenchallengeusa.org

14. Global Teen Challenge https://globaltc.org

15. Greater Piedmont Adult & Teen Challenge https://gpteenchallenge.com phone 336-292-7795 1912 Boulevard Street, Greensboro, NC 27407

RESOURCE OF FAITH-BASED RECOVERY SUPPORT GROUPS

ecarecounseling.com or greaterthanahigherpower.com